UML for Database Design

The Addison-Wesley Object Technology Series

Grady Booch, Ivar Jacobson, and James Rumbaugh, Series Editors
For more information check out the series web site [http://www.awl.com/cseng/otseries/].

The Component Software Series

Clemens Szyperski, Series Editor
For more information check out the series web site [http://www.awl.com/cseng/csseries/].

UML for Database Design

Eric J. Naiburg

Robert A. Maksimchuk

ADDISON–WESLEY

Boston • San Francisco • New York • Toronto • Montreal
London • Munich • Paris • Madrid
Capetown • Sydney • Tokyo • Singapore • Mexico City

The publisher offers discounts on this book when ordered in quantity for special sales. For more information, please contact:

Pearson Education Corporate Sales Division
One Lake Street
Upper Saddle River, NJ 07458
(800) 382-3419
corpsales@pearsontechgroup.com

Visit AW on the Web: www.awl.com/cseng/

Library of Congress Cataloging-in-Publication Data
Naiburg, Eric J.
    UML for database design / Eric J. Naiburg, Robert A. Maksimchuk.
        p. cm.
    Includes bibliographical references and index.
    ISBN 0-201-72163-5
    1. Database design. 2. UML (Computer science) I. Maksimchuk, Robert A. II. Title

QA76.9.D26 N35 2002
005.74–dc21

                                                              2001033569

0-201-72163-5
Text printed on recycled paper
1 2 3 4 5 6 7 8 9 10—MA—0504030201
First printing July 2001

*To my wife, Shelley, and my children,
Ken and Val. Thanks for your patience and
understanding during this long project.
Now things can get back to abnormal
around here. Love, Bob*

*To my wife, Karalyn, my son, Joseph,
and my daughter, Katherine, who arrived
partway through the process of writing
this book. Thank you for pushing me to continue
even when I wanted to slow down, for
understanding the importance of this project,
and for giving me my space when I needed
to get the work done. I love you all, Eric*

Contents

Foreword

My life would be vastly simpler if I were not awash in data.

My PDA is bursting at the seams with lists, spreadsheets, schedules, and documents that collectively enumerate, tabulate, quantify, and qualify my entire life (it's quite humbling to realize just how much of my life can fit in my shirt pocket). In turn, that PDA gets synchronized with my laptop, whose 16-gig drive is packed to capacity not just with applications but also with yet more lists, spreadsheets, schedules, and documents. My laptop is but one node in a local network of about a dozen machines that run my home and my office, and in each of them—no surprise—you'll find more lists, spreadsheets, schedules, and documents. Some of this data is unstructured—I'm not so driven that I maintain an XML representation of my grocery list (well, not yet . . .)—but much of that data is structured, semantically deep, and intermingled: tax records, code and related artifacts, catalogs of books and journals, reference materials for my in-progress manuscripts and presentations, catalogs of my CDs and associated play lists, and so on.

Step beyond this network, over which I have some degree of control, and it's frightening to think about all the data that people and organizations maintain about me: orders from Web sites; my college, military, and employment records; the government's tax records; and so on. Conservatively speaking, my digital life can probably be compressed into just a few gigabytes of memory. Multiply me by a few billion people, add data for everything other than personal information, and it's easy to see how some systems must cope with terabytes or even petrabytes of data. At the other end of the spectrum of complexity, even embedded devices must typically manage semantically rich data: for example, you'd be surprised to realize how much structured data something as truly embedded as a pacemaker must manipulate.

In short, virtually every interesting software-intensive system surrounds or manipulates a set of persistent data.

But therein lie a number of challenges: how do I craft a data-intensive system so that I can grow quality software around it? How do I architect that system so that it is resilient to change, realizing that, in many domains, kinds of data change relatively slowly but particular instances of information and applications that manipulate that information change much more frequently? Also, how do I organize my development team so that different stakeholders can work together, since some will be more skilled at designing the data-intensive parts of my system and others will be more skilled at crafting the applications that surround that data?

Eric and Robert together have deep experience in building data-intensive systems, and that experience is evident in their writing. They have written a soundly pragmatic book that addresses these issues and many more head on. Speaking of head on, there is often an unfortunate collision of worlds between the traditional database designers and application designers on a development team, but as the authors demonstrate, the use of the Unified Modeling Language permits these otherwise disparate groups to communicate with one another. Development is indeed a team sport, and integrating the data-intensive parts of a system with its application-intensive parts is critical.

The presence (or absence) of a well-crafted software architecture as well as an intentional process are clear predictors in the success (or failure) of many complex systems. Eric and Robert have thus organized this book along a life-cycle flow, leading you from conceptual to logical and then to physical database design. By focusing on a single, very rich case study, coupled with important observations for the database team highlighted in the sidebars, the authors offer guidance that can help your software development team succeed.

Grady Booch
Chief Scientist
Rational Software Corporation
April 2001

Preface

For database professionals, this book provides a practical guide to the use of the Unified Modeling Language (UML) for database design. It is intended for those who have to make things happen in the real world; those who have to deliver real systems to meet real business needs. In short, this book is designed for those pragmatic, working database designers who need to get things done.

UML for Database Design addresses the questions most frequently asked of us by database professionals from all over the globe:

- How can I use UML for database design in the real world?
- How can I fit the UML into my current process?
- How should the database design team adopt this approach?
- How can database and application teams work together using the UML?

The Approach

We have endeavored to ensure that this book didn't get lost in theory, buried in formalism, or trivialized by unrealistic, contrived examples. Thus, at times we may run contrary to the purists. That's OK. The approach we take is to introduce the use of UML for database design in a stepwise fashion, for each phase of the system development life cycle. We move from business modeling at the beginning of the life cycle to database design at the end. We show how the UML applies to the process and the value it provides to the database designer in each phase. A robust, realistic case study (described in Chapter 2) helps demonstrate how to use the UML and how to handle challenges that you may encounter during your real-world projects.

Chapter Summaries

Chapter 1—Introduction
This chapter indicates who should read this book and why. It describes the basic structure of subsequent chapters and the overall flow of the book.

Chapter 2—Database Design from Requirements to Implementation
This chapter discusses database modeling versus database design, addresses data modeling as it exists today, describes how using the UML differs from traditional techniques, and introduces the case study used throughout the remainder of the book.

Chapter 3—Business Modeling for Database Design
This chapter introduces business modeling and how it, and the UML, can be used for database design. Here is where the conceptual model is established.

Chapter 4—Requirements Definition
This chapter shows how all the artifacts provided by the previous business modeling are used to establish the system requirements.

Chapter 5—Analysis and Preliminary Design
This chapter moves from the realm of business requirements into the logical design of the system and its database.

Chapter 6—Preparing for Transformation to the Database Design Model
This chapter transitions from the logical analysis model to the database design model. This chapter also addresses the issues that arise during the mapping of object models to data models.

Chapter 7—Database Design Models—the UML Profile for Database Design
This chapter introduces the UML Profile for Database Design developed by Rational Software Corporation.

Chapter 8—Implementing the Physical Aspects of the Database
This chapter focuses on the physical component of database design.

Chapter 9—Summary of Using the UML for Database Design

This chapter performs a "postmortem" on how the UML was used in the case study project.

Appendix A—UML Models for EAB Healthcare, Inc.

This appendix contains the UML models from the case study project.

Appendix B—Use Case Descriptions

This appendix contains the use case descriptions from the case study project.

Acknowledgments

Thanks first to God without whom none of this would be possible.

Thanks to Paul Becker, Jessica Cirone, Elizabeth Ryan, and Ross Venables of Addison-Wesley for their invaluable assistance in the overall process.

Thanks to all our reviewers who kept us walking the straight and narrow path. A special thanks to Mike Engle, one of the best System Engineers and OO practitioners in the business. His thorough and relentless technical review added immensely to this book.

Thanks to Jim Conallen, Kevin Kelly, Terry Quatrani, Davor Gornik, Jeff Hammond, and Steve Rabuchin for their valued advice.

Thanks to Lisa Connelly and Mary Cicalese, who helped to make the opportunity for me (Eric) to move up in the world come true. Thanks also to Ed McLaughlin, who gave me the chance to prove myself; without that opportunity, I would not have the knowledge and skill to write this book.

Thank you to the people who have taken part on the data modeling team at Rational Software Corporation, without whom both of us would not have had the ability to prove our vision and see it come to life. This team includes Hong Lee Yu, Scott Schneider, Will Lyons, Tommy Fannon, Kingsley Wood, Barbara Evans, Larry Dunnell, Brian Lim, Bonnie St. John, Deborah Ford, Der Ping Chou, Douglas Robb, Hermant Kolwalkar, Ron DeWolfe, Rose Rosario, Susan Anstey, Teresa Dowling, Xiangmin Wang, Xiang (April) Li, Yi Gao, and Zoe Lin.

And a special thanks to Grady Booch and Jim Rumbaugh.

Contacts

We would appreciate your feedback on this book. If you have questions or comments, please feel free to contact us by email at gurus@UMLforDatabaseDesign.com, or visit our website *http://www.UMLforDatabaseDesign.com*.

Chapter 1

Introduction

Why Read This Book?

Systems Development Is a Team Sport

In today's business climate, systems development is a game that you can't afford to lose. Losing the game can literally cost you your entire business. Business analysis, software development, and database teams all need to work together to understand a business customer's problems and to solve them through the software systems they are assigned to create. We do not build systems just for the sake of keeping our jobs. There are valid business reasons for the systems. The typical overall goal is to make the business better (more efficient, more profitable, and so on). Sometimes the problem to solve lies not in the software but in the way a business process is performed. You may be improving infrastructure, customer experience, internal experience, or some type of business process, but it is not just for the sake of adding or changing the systems. There are critical requirements that need to be met, and it is the responsibility of all teams involved to create the best and most economical solution to fulfill the requirements levied upon them by the business.

In most organizations today, the analysis, development, and database teams work for different managers, business units, or other business organizations. Although these teams are separate, they are all working toward a common goal and need to work together. We have witnessed situations where members of the different teams had to be introduced to each other by name during a meeting although they had been working on the same project for years. This is not a good scenario. It causes the communication of requirements, and especially changes to those requirements, to be lost, misinterpreted, or resolved differently by different groups.

Generally you are not just changing one part of the system but also adding different pieces to a constantly changing system as new requirements are uncovered. In other words, software development is an iterative process. As the developers build the applications, they uncover new requirements just as the database team uncovers new requirements when building the database. These all need to be communicated not only via documents but also visually through models. This enables these requirements to be traced to the different artifacts throughout the development cycle. However, in the past this could not be done easily since there was no common language for all the development teams to use.

The Unified Modeling Language

The Unified Modeling Language (UML) has quickly become the standard language used for modeling business and software application needs. Although it is the standard of the Object Modeling Group (OMG), the UML is not just for modeling object-oriented (OO) applications. A common misconception is that the UML is intended only for OO development and can't be used for other types. However, the UML was designed as a very flexible and customizable language. This allows for many different types of modeling, including models for understanding the business process, workflow of events, sequence of queries, applications, databases, architectures, and more.

Using the UML for database design allows the business and application teams who are already using the UML for their designs to share a common language and to communicate with the database team. A common problem is that business analysts and developers are building enterprise architectures without considering the data and how the data will be affected. Can the database capture the information that is being described? Are there existing systems that already address the business's needs but are unknown to other teams? Do items with the same names mean completely different things? All of these questions lead us to conclude that the database team should be involved at the beginning of the development process, taking part in the initial analysis and continuing all the way throughout the complete development life cycle. With the ability of the UML to design so many different visual models, you can encompass an entire application and database design using a single language that everyone can share.

While reading this book, you will learn the different types of UML diagrams and how they apply to the database world. You will also understand how other teams may be using these diagrams and how all the teams can share their work rather than working in separate silos, not communicating until it is too late.

Who Should Read This Book?

Many members of the software development team—managers, team leaders, systems analysts, data analysts, software developers, and database designers, among others—can benefit from the information presented in this book. As we mentioned earlier, systems development is a team sport.

Specifically, this book is designed using a role-centric approach with the database team in mind. It highlights the role of the database team, including the database designer/analyst and database administrator roles. We will address the full life cycle of database design: database development from requirements to tables to deployment. The intent is to help these members of the team ease their transition from modeling with entity-relationship notations to modeling with the UML.

However, if you want to understand how the UML can be used throughout the system development life cycle, whether from the database or application point of view, we believe this book will be of significant value to you.

This book does not teach the UML or database design from the ground up. There are numerous books and courses that do that very well. However, you do not need to be an expert in these areas since we will introduce the important concepts at a level that will enable you to understand the material.

How to Read This Book

Beginning in Chapter 3, the chapters are organized as explained in this section. Depending on your experience level you might choose to focus on specific areas of the discussion.

Chapter Organization

The first paragraph of each chapter provides a synopsis of that chapter's content. The remainder of each chapter is divided into six sections as described below.

The Workflow

The workflow section describes at a high level what needs to be done at this point in the development life cycle and the rationale behind these tasks. This section provides a focus that will be most helpful to the project manager or team leader. An overview of the UML elements used in this phase is included as well as practical advice for the manager of these tasks.

The Case Study Status

This book includes a realistic case study of a fictitious healthcare company, EAB Healthcare, and focuses on automating specific parts of the business. Examining each stage of the development of EAB's system will help illustrate the different types of UML models and how they can be applied to systems development.

This section connects the reader back with the case study used in this text. The intent here is to inform the reader of the progress made by the case study development team "between chapters."

The Concepts

This section introduces UML, object-oriented, database, and other concepts used in each chapter. This is not meant to be a full tutorial on any of these technical areas. There are many books available that provide in-depth information on each of these areas. This section provides just a basic reference that should be sufficient for understanding the subsequent material.

The Approach

This section is similar to "The Workflow" section but presents information at the practitioner (that is, the "worker-bee") level. More specifics appear on how to approach or perform the tasks in the workflow. The section describes what to do and how to do it. Practical advice is included as in the earlier section but this time at the practitioner level.

The Design

This section takes the form of a narrative about what is happening with the case study development team, describing the team members' trials and tribulations (and lessons learned) as they work on the project. The actual design and how the team got there are discussed. Samples of the actual model are interspersed in the text.

Summary

This section summarizes the main points of the chapter.

Database Designer Callout Boxes

These shaded areas of text, interspersed throughout the book, are used to highlight areas that should be of particular interest to the database designer.

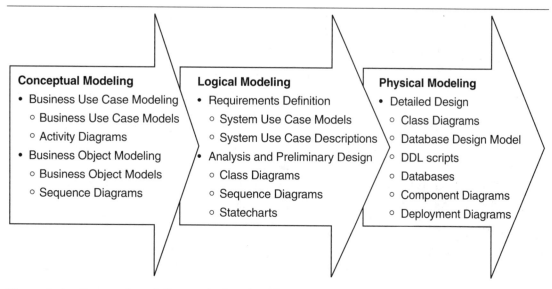

Conceptual Modeling
- Business Use Case Modeling
  - Business Use Case Models
  - Activity Diagrams
- Business Object Modeling
  - Business Object Models
  - Sequence Diagrams

Logical Modeling
- Requirements Definition
  - System Use Case Models
  - System Use Case Descriptions
- Analysis and Preliminary Design
  - Class Diagrams
  - Sequence Diagrams
  - Statecharts

Physical Modeling
- Detailed Design
  - Class Diagrams
  - Database Design Model
  - DDL scripts
  - Databases
  - Component Diagrams
  - Deployment Diagrams

Figure 1–1 Stages of modeling and related UML constructs

Process Flow Overview

The text and the associated case study progress through basic software development stages as depicted in Figure 1–1. Figure 1–1 shows an overview of the flow of the book in terms familiar to database designers and also in terms of the UML. Each level of modeling (conceptual, logical, and physical) shows within it the major activities performed and the key UML elements that support that activity. For example, in logical modeling, the analysis and preliminary design activities primarily use UML class, sequence, and statechart diagrams. Other UML elements may also be used but most of the activities will center on the noted elements.

One caveat—we have attempted to keep the approach described in this book as practical and pragmatic as possible. We are not theorists, nor academics, nor methodologists. We come from the real world of software development where "getting it done" is a major measure of success. Whenever we found theory colliding with practicality, we gave practicality the right of way.

Appendixes

You will find in the appendixes the actual UML models that were developed as part of the EAB Healthcare case study. For the interested student, these models provide an appreciation of the type and extent of models that would be developed for a system similar to that presented in the case study.

Chapter 2

Database Design from Requirements to Implementation

In this chapter we discuss the differences between traditional database modeling and database design, the UML diagrams that can be used for database design, and some of the differences between using the UML and more traditional techniques. We also explain the case study that will be used throughout the remainder of the book.

Database Modeling versus Database Design

Database Modeling

Database modeling is generally focused on logical and physical database models. A logical database model is composed of entities and attributes, and it includes relationships between the different entities, which can be mandatory or not. The logical model consists of a normalized model that is generally set to third normal form. It includes many elements that make up a database, but it is not specific to any software or database implementation. Performance factors are not a major consideration at this point nor are the applications that will be using the database. The main concern is building a model of what the database would look like when capturing the data needed by the users.

The denormalization process begins with the physical database model. The database team takes the work performed in the logical model and starts to optimize it for queries, specific database implementations, and applications that may talk to the database. More specific items, like views, are added to make working with the database easier for users. The physical database model also needs to be mapped back to the logical database model; they can be very different, and each has its own purpose. As changes occur, the team must update one model from the other and maintain that mapping between them.

Database Design

While *database modeling* focuses mostly on depicting the database, *database design* encompasses the entire process from the creation of requirements, business processes, logical analysis, and physical database constructs to the deployment of the database. For example, in database design, physical data modeling includes the modeling of not only tables and columns but also tablespaces, partitions, hardware, and the entire makeup of the database system. Database design includes uncovering and modeling requirements, the business processes (as they are today and where they are going in the future), the activities of the business, the logical models, and the physical database models, as well as addressing issues of what information is needed, how the different parts relate, how applications communicate with the data, and how the entire system is implemented.

Data Modeling Today

There are many tools and notations that address data modeling, but generally they are very focused on the implementation of the database. These tools and notations concentrate on logical and physical database modeling, usually ignoring other aspects of the business and its requirements. If you want to model and understand the business processes, requirements, and rules, you need additional tools and notations. If you want to understand the applications and how they relate to the database, once again you must move to other resources. This makes communication, reuse, and interoperability quite difficult, if not impossible.

There have been many methodologies, tools, and notations that championed different ways to best model, design, and build software applications from analysis through to database implementation. Some of these methodologies were very strict in the process and very tool intensive. If you wanted to customize these to fit how your organization did business, often you were out of luck. You had to do it the way prescribed by the tool or methodology. Since software development is an iterative process performed by different teams with different levels of experience and often in varying phases of the project's life cycle, it became quite difficult to work in such an environment. Working in such a linear path made it very difficult to accomplish work that needed to be done immediately without going through the other steps first. It was also quite difficult to go back and fill in some of the blanks once a step was skipped. The tools that support such a life cycle are often called *upper CASE tools* or *full life-cycle CASE tools*. Over time, people decided that a very strict methodology wasn't going to work in an environment that needed flexibility. They moved away from the upper CASE tools into what we call *lower CASE tools*. The organizations that moved to these types of tools and methodologies began to adopt best-of-breed solutions.

Best-of-Breed Solutions versus Full Life-Cycle Solutions

The majority of companies that moved to best-of-breed solutions have run into a new problem. How do the different teams involved in the development effort communicate requirements and changes? Using the full life-cycle tools and methodologies, although quite cumbersome, gave the business analyst, application developer, and database designer the ability to work together in the same environment with the same artifacts and information. Moving to a best-of-breed solution gives the different developers the ability to choose what is best for their subject matter but leaves the other teams behind. Often the business analyst is working with a documentation tool while the software developer is working with code or some UML models and the database designer is working with his or her own database modeling tools. The teams, which are working toward a common goal to solve a specific business problem, have now branched off into their own worlds and the door of communication has been slammed shut.

The relative inflexibility of the full life-cycle tools may have made doing an entire job difficult, but they at least brought the different teams together to solve the business problem that was placed before them. We have been involved with many companies that bring the business analysts, application developers, and database designers into a meeting and discover it's the first time they have met each other. The first question we ask in such a situation is, "If you don't even know each other and you are all working together to solve the same business problem, how do you communicate requirements, especially when they change?" The answers are usually the same. The company has some really large requirements document that gets updated occasionally and an e-mail goes out to notify everyone. For most people, this is a pretty difficult and ineffective way to communicate changes. We have never worked on a project that had no requirements changes from inception to the end of the project. (If there were a company with such projects, everyone would want to work there.) How can teams, sometimes with hundreds of people involved, communicate the requirements, especially if the requirements change often?

Using the full life-cycle tools, since everyone was working in the same environment, made it easy to communicate the requirements and their changes through some sort of repository or data dictionary that was common across the tool and methodology. But going to a best-of-breed solution has put an end to the common information. Often teams meet to define requirements for building enterprise architectures without taking into account the other teams that should be involved. Because the teams are using different tools and processes, they often create their own plans and architecture, which the teams then pass on to the other teams involved, many times causing wasted effort. If the analysts are working with the developers, for example, to build an enterprise architecture without bringing some of the database design team into the fold, there is a good chance that the architecture being designed will miss some important artifacts needed by the database team. We are not recommending that everyone from every team be involved in all meetings, but each team should be represented. This will help to avoid the problems of six different definitions for *customer* or architectures that have to be thrown away because the database that has been implemented can't support it.

A Happy Medium

Having full life-cycle tools hasn't proved to be a good answer for bringing teams together. Also, nobody likes a process that is so strict that they can't customize it to do what they want, when they want, and with the parts they want. The best-of-breed option has provided a good solution for individuals, but it ignores the fact that even though the reporting structures may be different and each person may be working on different parts of applications, everyone still needs to work together as a team and share information readily.

The UML has the best of both worlds. There are many tools like Rational Rose, which will support the life cycle using the UML, yet they are flexible enough to do what you want when you need it. Using the UML as a language for the entire life cycle of the development effort allows all of the teams involved to work together in one way but to do their own part as needed. Since the UML is "process agnostic," its use can be altered as needed to fit into your company's structure and processes.

UML Diagrams for Database Design

There are many types of UML diagrams available to help database designers do their jobs. These diagrams can be used for capturing requirements, depicting deployment, and everything in between. The different UML diagram types are listed in Table 2-1.

Table 2-1   Descriptions of the UML Diagrams

Diagram	Description
Use case	The use case diagram is a model of the system's intended functions and its environment that supports the business processes. This model serves as a contract between the customer and the developers.
Interaction	Interaction diagrams are either sequence or collaboration diagrams, both of which show the interaction of objects within the system. They can be used to understand queries that will affect the database and even help build indexes based on the information modeled.
Activity	Activity diagrams show the flow of a process. They can be used to show a high-level view of the business and how it operates.
Statechart	Statecharts capture the dynamic behavior of the system or objects within the system.
Class	Class diagrams are logical models that show the basic structure of the system.
Database	The database diagram depicts the structure of the database including tables, columns, constraints, and so on.
Component	Component diagrams show the physical storage of the database, including the database management system, tablespaces, and partitions. They can also include applications and their interfaces used to access a database.
Deployment	Deployment diagrams show the hardware configuration that is used for the database and applications.

Why Use the Various UML Diagrams?

UML modeling has come into mainstream use through the pathway of object-oriented analysis and design (OOAD), but it can be used for many different types of analysis and design modeling without ever building object-oriented applications. Development of the language was driven by the need to understand object-oriented development and how the architecture of a project affects the outcome. However, don't exclude the use of the UML just because you are not building object-oriented applications—the UML can be used for basically any type of analysis and design project, whether or not the database or systems are object oriented, even outside of software. An example of this is an auto manufacturer that models the way its cars are assembled, particularly the specifications of the parts that third-party vendors supply. The company uses these UML models for quality control and to provide the models to prospective vendors who are bidding to build a specific part.

Being able to visualize the requirements helps the development team understand more easily and quickly the impacts of changes. Having models like use cases and activity diagrams helps the teams examine such questions as, "What will happen if . . . ?" It is much easier for people to understand a quick picture that shows who will do activity x, then y, then z, rather than trying to read numerous paragraphs of text that describe the same information. Textual descriptions can be interpreted differently by the different people who are reading them.

The goal of using the UML for business processes, application development, and database modeling is to tie development teams together and make sure that organizations no longer build enterprise architectures without involving all teams that are important to the process. Building a team that is cross functional with the specific areas of expertise helps create an architecture that can be built and supported by all parties involved. If the different teams work in isolated silos, they eventually lose touch with the rest of the project. In many situations, individuals uncover new requirements, but often this information is not fed back into the overall project. As changes occur throughout the project life cycle, the UML diagrams can be updated so that everyone involved can understand the changes impacting their respective areas.

Sometimes just the diagrams are not enough. Metadata is very important to describe what has been modeled. Making sure, for example, that the word *customer* means the same to all groups and isn't used in different ways is critical. You need to do a very good job of capturing this ancillary information. Again, this is where having everybody working in one language and notation helps. From the beginning, you can all get together to build the initial requirements and develop an early understanding of what *customer* means before breaking off into separate teams to begin deeper analysis and design in your specific areas.

Also, with the use of stereotypes, you can extend the UML to fit your needs even more specifically. A stereotype is a UML modeling element that extends the existing elements within the UML metamodel without directly changing the metamodel. Stereotyping a UML element causes it to act as something else, and by acting as that new element it has specific properties. To put it in database terms, for example, consider a table as the base element. When you stereotype it as an entity, this table now behaves as an entity and has attributes instead of columns. However, in the metamodel they are mapped to the same place. You may also add some additional tagged values based on the stereotype, which are then added to the metamodel.

The UML Differs from Traditional Database Modeling

Traditional database modeling promotes the basic theory that the database is the backbone of the system and everything revolves around that database.

Although it is true that much—if not most—of the important information of the organization lives within the database, the database cannot stand on its own, and there are many other things that make up the company and its information. Without the applications to open the database to employees, there would be no accessible data. Without customers and transactions, there would be no information for the database. Without a business for which to build the database, there would be no reason to have a database. For these and many other reasons, the database must exist together with the rest of the organization and must be considered just one piece of the puzzle that must coexist with all the others.

The previous statement may seem obvious, but it is not evidenced in many of the companies we have worked in and visited. The database team often works on its own without open doors of communication. The information it captures is based on the database the team members are building and not the entire system that is needed. The blame should not be put onto the database team, though; the tools and methodologies that support the different types of design have led the database team down this road, and most people have not yet begun to move outside of the box into which they have been put. Using the most commonly available tools and the most prevalent methodologies, organizations have chosen to split the teams involved in requirements definition, development, and database management, enforcing the barriers and making communication difficult.

Bringing in the UML enables a common language for all teams involved and starts to break down those walls, reuniting people into one development team. Traditional database modeling concerns itself mainly with the database. The database is very important, and you must concentrate on your subject matter area. The problem begins when people focus so hard on their subject matter areas that they don't think outside of that subject and don't even communicate beyond their walls. Bringing a common language like the UML into the mix doesn't require you to do your database modeling differently—it just means that the database modeling that you are doing today must expand outside of just the database structures and become a part of the entire analysis and design process.

In the process that we follow throughout this book, we explore the various parts of the development process, focusing on the job of the database analyst and designer. Using the UML doesn't inhibit the way that you traditionally design the database, although the notations may look a little different compared with the familiar old ones. When designing the database with the UML, you still have tables, columns, triggers, constraints, and the other elements that you generally use when modeling and designing a database. They just may be described a little bit differently and will definitely be more easily communicated to the rest of the teams involved with the development process.

The UML gives you the ability to model, in a single language, the business, application, database, and architecture of the systems. By having one single language, everybody involved can communicate their thoughts, ideas, and requirements. As described earlier, you can use the parts of the UML that are pertinent to your job and not be left out when other teams do their tasks. Also, by using the UML, you can always go back in the process to update information and include new information that may be discovered or required later.

In this book, we cover the different ways to model during the life cycle of database design and how the different teams can work together to accomplish common goals through modeling. By having all teams working together to understand and define the business, uncover needed changes, prioritize those changes, and model the business, they can all understand the job ahead. This will also help them recognize changes to the requirements as the project proceeds to ensure that each team takes advantage of changes made by others and to successfully use the changes that are made.

The Case Study

In the book, we follow a case study of a fictitious company, EAB Healthcare, Inc., to demonstrate how they began to understand their business systems, how they made changes to those systems to better serve their customers (both internal and external), and how they designed new elements in their database to best serve their purposes.

EAB Healthcare is a fictional provider of physical rehabilitation and nursing care to older adults. While traditional healthcare facilities are suffering financial difficulties and are undergoing industry-wide consolidation, EAB has been tremendously successful. This is primarily due to their innovative rehabilitative therapy programs and their focus on efficient facility operation.

In an effort to remain a leader in their industry through improving their operational excellence, EAB has undertaken a project to computerize the vast volume of paper medical records that all of their nationwide facilities must handle on a daily basis.

The Vision

The business client's ultimate vision for this project is to have a fully automated, online medical records system that will

- Eliminate the need to manually handle the large volume of paper medical records by providing these records in electronic form
- Fully integrate their records into a medical records database

- Enforce regulatory record-keeping requirements
- Eliminate the manual transcription of information between currently paper-based information sets

The desired outcome is improved patient care through better information management and more effective staff operations.

A Typical Scenario

Using the new system, the staff of EAB will typically access the medical records via touch-sensitive information display panels that will be present in each resident's room, in all treatment areas, and in all staff offices. The following describes a typical usage scenario.

> A nurse enters a resident's room to assess the resident's status. Noticing the resident's trend toward excessive weight loss, the nurse needs to review the patient's dietary orders in the medical records. She goes to the informational display and swipes her personal access card. Once recognized by the system, she enters her personal identification number (PIN). Security verification allows her to access the system. She enters the resident's name and the system displays the resident's records to her. (Depending on the person's role, the system may grant access as read-only, read/write, read/write/create/destroy, or other appropriate combinations. The system may also make available only certain sections of the medical records, also established by role.) The nurse finds and reviews the information she needs. She then ends her session with the system.

The Project Goals

The ultimate business goals for this project are as follows:

1. To reduce errors and improve the accuracy of the medical records
2. To improve efficiency by reducing the amount of physical paper the workers handle in daily operations
3. To streamline the interaction between the EAB facilities and the myriad external regulatory agencies and other private service providers with whom EAB interacts

Due to their commitment to quality and since there is such intense oversight of the healthcare industry by external government agencies, EAB has committed to a thorough analysis and design of this new system. The process will begin with business modeling, then system analysis and design using the UML and object-oriented techniques.

Our Focus

We use this case study throughout the book to illustrate how such a system may be developed using UML-based techniques. However, we focus primarily on the database design aspects of the project, not on the development of the application software. Thus, while many of the designs in this book may address application issues, we ultimately focus on the database design supporting the EAB Healthcare system.

Chapter 3

Business Modeling for Database Design

In this chapter we look at the different types of UML diagrams that can be used to model a business, focusing on the way that EAB Healthcare operates today. Subsequent chapters expand upon these models to depict the changes that could occur in the future based on the vision for the business's growth.

The Workflow

Understanding a company and its business is a very difficult task. You need to understand what the company does and the activities involved, what information exists, who the customers and partners are, and much more. You need to understand not only the company's business today but also the direction it is going and its vision over both the short and long term.

Most organizations have no standard way to describe their business in detail and, especially, no way to model the business. However, there are several types of business models and various notations and methodologies available for use in modeling a business. There are also many different items that you may want to model, for example, the business processes, workflows, activities, interactions with other businesses, partners, customers, systems, and even the rules according to which the business runs.

Whether you work within the company or as an outside consultant, when you look at the company you can begin to understand the major mission of the business and how things operate. However, without spending a good amount of time talking with many of the different members of the company, you will not be able to understand the drivers and processes of the business. From the shipping clerk to the CEO, you need to retrieve information on how they think the business works and how they do their jobs. It is very important to interview more than one person in each role if possible to get a good understanding of the business and the ways different employees perform particular roles. You are looking for some basic information:

- How the workers see the business
- What they believe the company really does to be successful
- What they believe the company is doing wrong
- How the individuals perform their activities

Additional items to consider, which we cover in later chapters, include specific rules about the business. The business rules are very important, and while working to understand the business at this stage many of these rules may be captured. However, they are more useful later when we move into the design phase.

Business Modeling

The best way to understand the information you obtain from the many players is to begin modeling their descriptions. Being able to visualize the business rather than just reading words can be very helpful. We begin with use case diagrams. A business use case diagram is a diagram of the intended functions of the business and is used in business modeling as an essential input to identify roles and deliverables in the organization [Leffingwell and Widrig 2000]. The business model should include both internal and external views and generally is composed of several different diagrams to show the different parts of the business.

Use case diagrams contain actors and use cases (Figure 3-1). Actors are anyone or anything that may interact with the business. Use cases define a series of actions that benefit the initiating actor or actors.

For the case study, we will look at EAB Healthcare's business by using use case diagrams. Some examples of business actors at EAB are Auditors, Physicians, Medical Supply Vendors, Residents, and External Service Providers (Figure 3-2). As you can see, these are many of the people, companies, and even systems that work with and for EAB as well as the people who are supported by EAB, such as the Residents.

In business modeling, you want to look at not only which groups participate in the business but also how the participants work. By showing the basic workflow of a business, activity diagrams allow analysts to understand how people do their jobs and which systems and processes they follow. Activity dia-

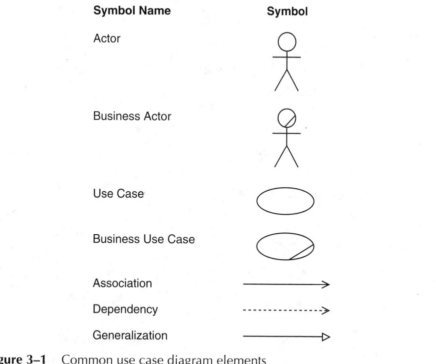

Symbol Name	Symbol
Actor	
Business Actor	
Use Case	
Business Use Case	
Association	
Dependency	
Generalization	

Figure 3–1   Common use case diagram elements

grams are a basic workflow of how a business works. They can be nontechnical, allowing everyone involved in creating the system, from the business users to the highly technical staff members, to understand the information. You can think of an activity diagram as a sophisticated flowchart. Figure 3-3 shows the elements commonly used in activity diagrams, and Figure 3-4 shows a sample activity diagram.

Activity diagrams drill down on the specific use cases to allow a reader to understand more deeply how the use cases are accomplished. Activity diagrams serve many purposes, including

- Understanding the business as it exists today
- Identifying areas of the business to be changed
- Discovering redundancies in the business processes
- Discovering bottlenecks in the business processes
- Identifying activities that could be better performed internally or externally
- Establishing the information needs of a particular activity or business use case

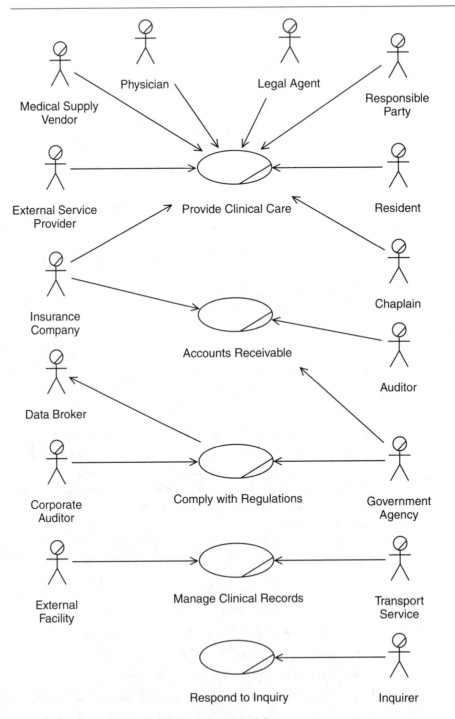

Figure 3–2 Sample business use case model

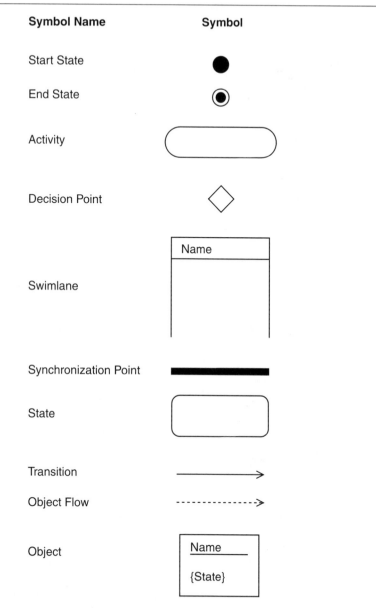

Figure 3–3   Common activity diagram elements

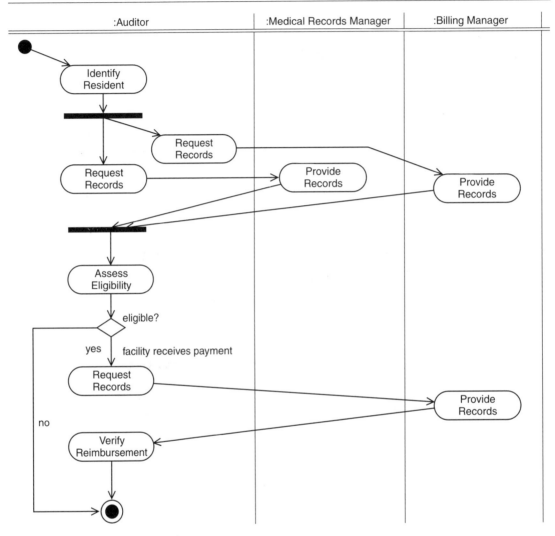

Figure 3–4   Sample activity diagram

When building the activity diagrams or any type of analysis diagrams, you must be sure not to fall into what is known as *analysis paralysis*. Analysis paralysis is the process of spending so much time and energy analyzing the business that you never get past the analysis phase. It is very important to understand when to cut off the analysis and begin designing the systems. You can and will always revisit the analysis phase during the other phases when following an iterative approach. New requirements and processes are uncovered routinely while building the system.

The Business Today

Through understanding the business and how it works today, you will begin to understand the systems and how they work (or don't work) as well. During this phase the business models help you start to see activities that are repetitive, systems that are overused, and systems that are not used to their potential for whatever reason. When looking at the entire business there is also a need to understand what processes, systems, software, hardware, and so on already exist. The point of this is to understand not only the current business but also, as it moves forward, how to improve it. If there are things that can be changed manually in the way the company does business, great, but the problems we are looking to uncover are those to be solved by software that supports the business. In the case study, we use the business models being created to understand how the company operates along with the knowledge of what systems are used. Once this is completed, subsequent chapters begin to explore where the business will go next and what needs to be changed to allow it to evolve to the next level.

Current Systems

When looking at the systems, you must look not only at the tangible items like hardware and software but also at the people (the actor roles) you have in place to support, build, and utilize the tangibles. By looking at the actors in the use cases and the activities performed in those use cases, you can understand where the company is lacking in resources, over-resourced, or perfectly fulfilled. By modeling the entire business and the processes around that business, you can look at the big picture and understand the successes, shortfalls, and needs of an organization. Use of the UML for this modeling allows the entire team to work together by standardizing a way to capture the information, tie the requirements to systems, update the models as things change, and understand the effects on the rest of the environment. Use case and activity diagrams help define the current systems, knowledge of which is very important for moving through the analysis of the business.

Today's Systems at Work

Knowing the systems is the first step, but there is also a need to understand the systems' details. People reading the different UML diagrams, such as use case and activity diagrams, can begin to understand how the systems are used. Use case diagrams show what processes are in place. For example, you can model the different systems as actors. Use cases interact with these systems through relationships to the representative actors. Activity diagrams show how the use cases are fulfilled. By drilling down to the specific ways the use cases are handled, the creators of the diagram can show exactly the steps and systems used to fulfill a specific use case or group of use cases. This allows the teams to understand the workings of the systems, indicating where there may be delays, underusage, and problems with the process.

Some tools offer the ability to run activity diagrams through a simulation. The simulation allows teams to view how the systems actually work, showing the different components of the activities, and through the input of rules and past experiences the tools can calculate the time processes take, predict bottlenecks, reveal inconsistencies, and more. By tweaking the activities, simulations can help predict how such changes will affect the activities and possibly even make recommendations for future changes. Having the ability to view a simulation is not crucial, but it can be quite helpful for understanding today's systems and the effects of changes in the business, business rules, or systems.

The Case Study Status

Speaking from the perspective of the teams involved in the case study, this is the first time we will build diagrams to understand EAB Healthcare's business. Previously we learned some basic information about EAB Healthcare: what the company does, how some of the employees work, and what some of the main jobs and positions are. In this chapter, we begin to understand the details of the business and its processes. EAB Healthcare wants to handle its clinical records electronically, and we will use the UML to understand EAB's business processes specific to clinical records. The different types of UML diagrams allow us to understand how the business works and its processes as well as EAB's strengths and weaknesses. Modeling the business, rather than just reading documents, makes it easier to understand how process changes will affect the business. As we attempt to understand how the business is running, we will uncover ways to change the business and its systems to improve EAB Healthcare, making the company more profitable and providing better service for customers.

The Concepts

This section introduces UML, object-oriented, database, and other concepts (such as the business modeling concepts, which are based on the Rational Unified Process developed by Rational Software Corporation). For a more complete discussion and more rigorous definitions of UML concepts, see Booch et al. [1999].

Actor—an external person or system that interfaces with (that is, uses or is used by) the system

Use case—a complete flow of actions, initiated by an actor, that the system performs to provide value to that actor

Business actor—an actor that is external to the business

Business use case—a use case, initiated by a business actor, that the business performs

Business worker—an actor that is internal to the business whose work helps realize a business use case

Business entity—something used by a business worker when fulfilling a use case

Business model—a model that describes the business operation, composed of the business use case model and the business object mode

Business use case model—a use case model that describes the business functions from a business actor's point of view; an external view of the business

Business object model—an object model that provides the realization of a business use case; an internal view of the business

Use case diagram—a diagram that shows use cases and their relationships with actors and other use cases

Class diagram—a diagram that shows classes, their interrelationships, and their relationships with other model elements

Sequence diagram—a diagram of collaborating objects and the messages they send to each other, arranged in time order, that shows how use cases are realized

Association—a relationship between two model elements

Generalization—a relationship between model elements indicating that one element (subclass) is a "type of" another element (superclass)

Aggregation—a relationship between model elements indicating that one element is a "part of" another element (aggregate)

The Approach

Involving the Database Team

Using the UML to capture business requirements lends a tremendous benefit to everyone on the database team, including the data analyst, database administrator, data modeler, and any others who work directly or indirectly with the database.

By using the UML as a common language among the analysis, development, and database teams and working together to understand the requirements and create the use case models of the business, you can best learn how the business works and what type of information needs to be captured. Data is the most important artifact of the majority of organizations that exist today. It includes most financial, customer, employee, and product information along with a variety of other information that allows a business to continue to work on a daily basis.

In many organizations, business analysis is done without at least consulting the database community or even taking the data into account. This is a recipe for disaster. Without working closely with the database community when building enterprise architectures, you cannot effectively model and understand the business. The database teams need to participate in the capture of business requirements and the process of understanding the current and potential future business goals to be sure that what the group believes is needed by the business can be accommodated by database services. We have seen many system requirements built and even applications begun fail because the database team's view was never considered. Having all teams participate from the beginning ensures that every point of view is considered. This does not mean that 40 people must gather in a room to come up with requirements; however, each stakeholder in the project should be represented. The involvement of each team in understanding the business processes will allow each one to suggest ways to build the architecture for the system to solve the business problems that are uncovered. Not having all necessary teams involved will cause a breakdown of communication and the development of an architecture that doesn't meet all parties' needs.

For database designers, working on a project this early in the system life cycle may be an unusual experience. Therefore, the focus of business modeling must be kept in mind at all times. How does the current business function? How does your customer want the business to function in the future? (Whether the customer is the actual end user of the system being built or the business people in your company who are responsible for having the system built for that end user, or both, depends on the structure of your business.) At this point, the emphasis is on the business processes and not the hardware, software, and manual operations that will implement these new processes. This poses a dilemma for the designers. Since we must understand the current business, people will naturally discuss the current business in terms of existing hardware, applications, and databases with which they are familiar. This type of discussion has an important place in business modeling, but we must not allow it to redirect the team away from the key question: What must the new system do? How the system will perform its functions is determined much later during the design phase.

Eliciting the Business Needs

The analysts should approach business modeling as a cooperative effort among themselves and the business people. This usually will take the form of meetings to elicit the needs of the business. Joint Application Development (JAD) sessions help the group understand the business. JAD is the process of bringing project participants together in structured group brainstorming sessions to define requirements, gather essential information, and make critical decisions. JAD results in faster discovery and enhances analysis and decision making by uncovering the information needed from various points of view. In this process, individuals or groups sit together and have an open, free-flowing discussion of ideas, which requires detailed note taking and modeling of some of the discussion on the fly.

Often there will be much heated discussion among the business people about what the business really does and how the various functions are performed. This is not to be discouraged. This is not an indicator that they don't understand the business. It is more likely they've never had to explain all the intricacies in detail before. Let the discussion continue awhile before you refocus the meeting. You don't want to build the wrong system just to avoid some temporary discomfort or embarrassment.

Set the expectation that many short meetings will be needed to refine the business model. In fact, to make the most of the business people's time, you may choose not to do any modeling during these sessions. You may just gather as much information as possible and do the actual modeling later. This often depends on whether the business people are amicable to the idea of modeling. Don't try to model the entire business in one meeting. In fact, it is unlikely that you will need to model the entire business at all, unless you are tasked with Business Process Reengineering. Business modeling is more focused and narrower in scope. As you proceed with your modeling many questions will arise. Your models will change greatly as your understanding of the business needs evolves. Be assured that this is normal, but sometimes it disturbs those in charge. You need to get long-term buy-in from the business people for this process to be successful.

Your goals for business modeling are varied. You should strive to understand the existing business. You may or may not choose to model the existing business. In this case study, the goal is automation of the existing paper-based records system; therefore, knowing the existing business is important. You must understand the business needs that are driving each specific development project. Those needs will drive the development of the new business model. The information you elicit in the brainstorming sessions should provide you with ample knowledge to create a conceptual data model. The conceptual data model will contain the key data entities, their names, their relationships with each other, and possibly some critical attributes and/or candidate keys.

The Design

From the problem statement provided and interviews with numerous staff people at EAB Healthcare, it became apparent that the company's goal is not to redesign all of the business processes. We are not doing Business Process Reengineering. The business people want to focus only on those parts of the business that use the clinical records. As a result, in the business model, you won't see the human resources, facility maintenance, accounts payable, or other key business processes at EAB. The focus is on the main process of the business—providing resident care.

The Business Use Case Model

The first part of the business model is the business use case model, which focuses on how the business is viewed by external actors and their interactions with the business. The external actors, which can be people or systems, are known as business actors. One of the earliest discussions with EAB was to identify these business actors. The results are shown in Figure 3-5.

This business use case model shows the business actors (the stick figures with slashes), the business use cases (the ovals with slashes), and the associations between them (the arrows). It is a very simple model showing which business actors interface with (that is, use) which business use cases. Once again we must stress the importance of keeping the modeling effort in context. These obviously are not all the actors that participate in some way to render resident care. For example, Ken, who works in the kitchen, provides a form of resident care. However, he is not involved with the clinical records system in any way. Therefore, he is not included in this model.

Each of these business actors has a textual description in the model. Some are self-evident, such as Physician, Chaplain, Insurance Company, and so on. Some are not, such as Data Broker (a contractor to government agencies who provides various data analysis functions) and Resident (whom laypeople would call "the patient"—the person receiving the wonderful care EAB provides). The Resident is interesting; we have represented this actor in the model as a business actor. This implies the Resident is external. But since this is a person who lives in the EAB Healthcare facility, it would seem natural to consider this actor to be internal—and this would be incorrect. The Resident does use the system, as we shall see later. Also, EAB does provide services to the Resident. The Resident actor is indeed external—a business actor.

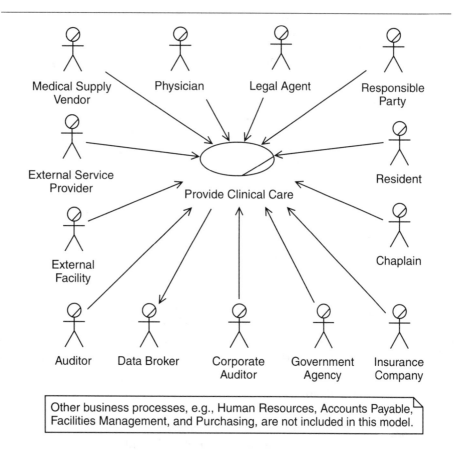

Figure 3–5 Overview business use case model for EAB Healthcare

Whether or not these business actors' definitions are self-evident to the business people with whom you are working, each business actor should be given a definition. The people who eventually build this system may not have a full understanding of what these self-evident business actors are or do. Even the most seemingly obvious actors may need some explanation. For example, the Physician in this model is external to EAB. This is not to imply that EAB has no physicians on staff. Some will and some will not be on staff. However, the status of their employment is not the issue here. The Physicians are external users of the business system modeled here. For example, a Physician may request a Resident's clinical records. An internal worker, the Medical Records Manager, may fulfill this external request. Such key distinctions need to be captured.

Finally, notice that the model in Figure 3-5 is referred to as an *overview* business use case model [Jacobson et al. 1995]. This is because the use case

Provide Resident Care represents a huge business function with many different business processes. Provide Resident Care will actually be realized by a number of other business use cases that are more limited in scope. Note that this does not imply functional decomposition. This is merely a higher level of abstraction that allows us to understand the overall context.

So what are the business use cases that realize Provide Resident Care? Further discussion with the EAB staff yields over 30 potential business use cases. That number is far too high for this one part of EAB's overall business, so we have to "WAVE" some away. That is, we apply the following tests:

W Does the use case describe **W**hat to do and not how?

A Is the use case described from the **A**ctor's viewpoint?

V Does the use case include **V**alue for the actor?

E Is the flow of events an **E**ntire business process?

Many of the initial "business use cases" that come up during discussion are merely one or two steps in a longer process. We include these in larger business use cases. Some are minor variants of the same actions. These we make common to be used by other business use cases. The ones that had no or little value are either deleted or added to other business use cases, respectively. Those that are focused on systems or implementation, instead of one or more actors, are eliminated. The results are shown in Figure 3-6.

Here we see a more refined and manageable view of the business. Also, during this activity, new business actors are added—Transport Service (companies that provide transportation of the Resident, and clinical records, to and from the EAB Healthcare facility) and Inquirer (someone inquiring on the condition of the Resident). This kind of discovery happens often in iterative design. This is not a sign of omission but a sign of gaining a deeper understanding of the business.

The Provide Clinical Care business use case is the process of providing day-to-day medical care for the residents. The Accounts Receivable business use case is a billing function that uses the clinical records to determine the amount of reimbursement owed to the facility. Comply with Regulations is the business use case that EAB must perform in order to have government approval to operate as a business. (This is a critical business process. The staff actually spends as much time handling all the paperwork to ensure compliance as they do providing medical care to the Residents.) Manage Clinical Records is the record management and maintenance business process. Respond to Inquiry is the constant process of the staff answering questions about the Residents and the care they are receiving. All of these business use cases must be performed properly as part of Provide Resident Care (the overview business use case).

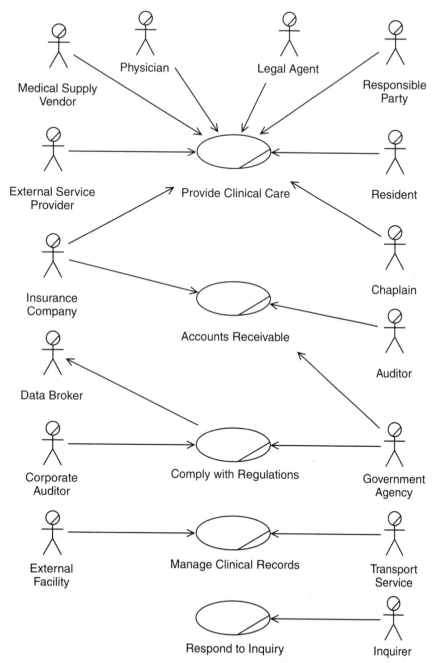

Figure 3–6 Business use case model to Provide Resident Care

To complete the business use case model, we must elaborate the business flow in each of the business use cases. Activity diagrams depict the flow of the business process and who is performing the various parts of the process. A key factor to remember when modeling a business is to describe the business process from the viewpoint of the business actor. While this may sound simple, the business actors do not see all the "behind-the-scenes" activities that are performed to serve their needs. Therefore, the internal details of the business functions are not included in these activity diagrams. As you discuss the flow of these business use cases with the business people, they will probably provide you with both external and internal details. You must take care to avoid adding internal details at this level. A simple example of an activity diagram is shown in Figure 3-7.

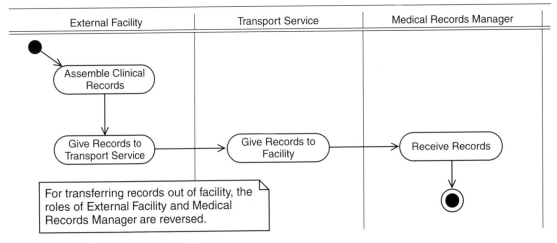

Figure 3–7 Activity diagram to Transfer Records to the facility

■ Database Designer

As a designer you can get your first look into the initial components of a conceptual data model. Even at this early point, from the business use case model you can see information that probably will need to be in the database—for example, clinical records, residents, physicians, and accounts. Also, some access and processing information is available—the External Facility, Transport Service, and Medical Records Manager all have access to the clinical records. The Medical Records Manager receives the records. The term *receives* should cause you to question what *receives* means. This is a natural part of the requirement elicitation process.

This simple activity diagram shows the process flow of transferring the clinical records from the point of view of the business actors (External Facility and Transport Service). The "swimlanes," vertical columns in the activity diagram, divide the diagram into areas of responsibility. In Figure 3-7, the External Facility is responsible for assembling the clinical records and giving the records to the Transport Service. The Transport Service's only responsibility is to give the records to the Facility. The ovals represent the activities that the various actors must perform. The arrows indicate the flow of the overall process, starting at the solid circle and ending at the outlined circle.

This business process, from the view of the business actors (External Facility and Transport Service) ends when the Medical Records Manager, who is an internal business worker—not a business actor—receives the records. The business actors do not see what the Medical Records Manager does with the records or any of the other internal workings of the business.

A slightly more complex activity diagram is shown in Figure 3-8. This shows the Provide Clinical Care process from the viewpoint of an External Care

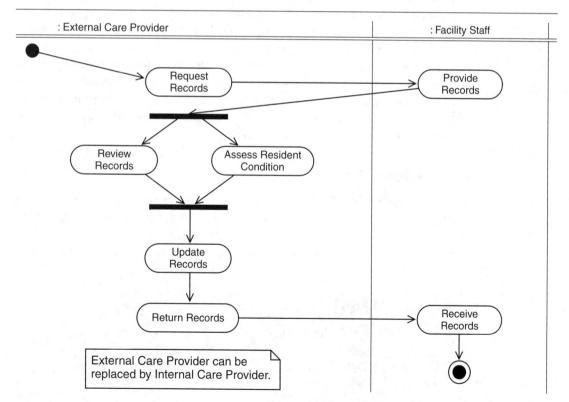

Figure 3–8   Activity diagram for the Provide Clinical Care use case

> ■ **Database Designer**
>
> The activity diagram shown in Figure 3–8 provides more insight to the conceptual data. We now see that the External Care Provider can review (read), update, and return (send) the clinical records. The Facility Staff can provide (send) and receive the clinical records.

Provider (includes External Service Providers, External Facilities, Physicians, and Medical Supply Vendors). Note the addition of the synchronization points, represented as horizontal bars. These indicate points at which the process flow splits into independent flows or comes together (synchronizes) into a single flow.

The activity diagram for the Accounts Receivable business use case, Figure 3–9, adds a new construct—the decision point (shown as a diamond). This is where the Auditor determines the eligibility for payment for the treatment received. Here we also see that the Auditor interfaces with two other actors, the Medical Records Manager and the Billing Manager.

Once the remaining activity diagrams are completed, the business use case model is done. But just a word of warning about being "done": at this point in the iterative analysis and design process, nothing is "done" for long. It is not unusual for important distinctions to be revealed at a later stage of analysis and design. This often causes a backward ripple, impacting the previous work you thought was "complete." This can be frustrating to the designer and outright frightening to management. Be assured that this is a normal phenomenon to which you will become accustomed in time.

The Business Object Model

The other part of the business model is the business object model, which focuses on how the people inside the business (business workers) accomplish the business processes. This is an inside look at how the business workers interact with other business workers, business actors, and business entities to

> ■ **Database Designer**
>
> In the activity diagram shown in Figure 3–9, we find new conceptual data—billing records and reimbursement records. Also, note that *eligibility* may be a possible attribute (that is, column) of a *treatment* (another candidate data entity). As before, we also see which business actors can manipulate this data.

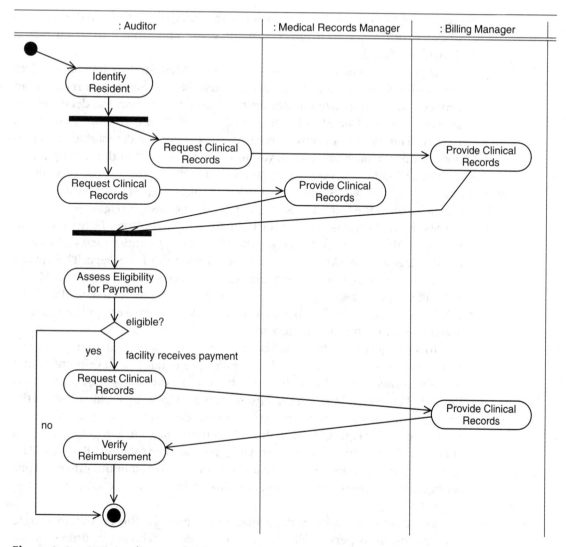

Figure 3–9 Activity diagram for the Accounts Receivable use case for reimbursement

achieve the business processes (that is, business use cases) that were just defined in the business use case model.

The first component of the business object model is a class diagram that contains the business actors, business workers (a slashed circle with an arrow, containing a stick figure), business entities (a slashed circle with a flat base), and their associations with each other needed to accomplish the respective business use case. The business use case gives you the starting point for the business object model, that is, it gives you the external entities and the business workers with which to begin. The simplest example from EAB Healthcare is shown in Figure 3-10.

Only one business entity needed to be added for this business object model—the Clinical Records. While this class diagram shows the relationship between the appropriate entities for this business use case, the details of the internal processes need to be described as well. This can be done using an activity diagram. However, we prefer to use a sequence diagram for this purpose. Sequence diagrams enable you to be more detailed in the description of the process. Little is needed to explain the internal workings of the very simple Respond to Inquiry business use case. When asked a question, the Facility Staff merely looks in the Clinical Records to provide the answer (Figure 3-11).

Sequence diagrams are read vertically, from top to bottom. Time flows from the top to the bottom of the page. The participating entities (actors, business entities, business workers, and so on) are at the top of the page. The arrows depict the messages or requests that flow between these entities. In Figure 3-11, the Inquirer asks a question of the Facility Staff. The Facility Staff gets the Clinical Records, looks for the answers, provides the answers to the Inquirer, and then returns the Clinical Records.

To show just how much valuable information can be elicited from even simple business object models, let us follow, in detail, the development of a business object model that is just a bit more complex—Manage Clinical Records. Let's begin building the business object model by looking back at the Manage Clinical Records business use case model's activity diagram for transferring records (Figure 3-7). From this activity diagram we get two actors (External Facility and Transport Service), one worker (Medical Records Manager), and one business entity (Clinical Records) involved in the process. Thus we begin the business object model for this business use case as shown in Figure 3-12.

As we proceed to build the sequence diagram for this seemingly simple flow, the business person tells us that for Residents who are returning to the

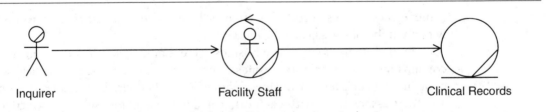

Figure 3–10   Business object model for the Respond to Inquiry business use case

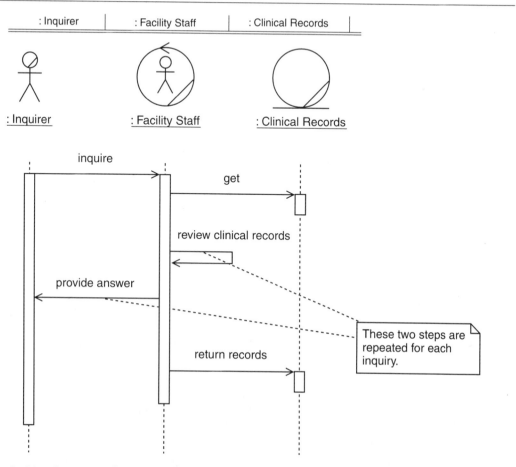

Figure 3–11 Sequence diagram for the Respond to Inquiry business use case

---

■ **Database Designer**

So why bother building the sequence diagram for such a simple process? Even this simple sequence diagram provides needed information to the database designer. The Clinical Records must be accessed by the Facility Staff (read-only), the Facility Staff needs to be able to search through the records (a query), and the records must be returned. (And what does *returned* mean? Does this mean *released*, as in releasing a lock that was put on the records?) Also, note that the Inquirer does *not* get access to the records.

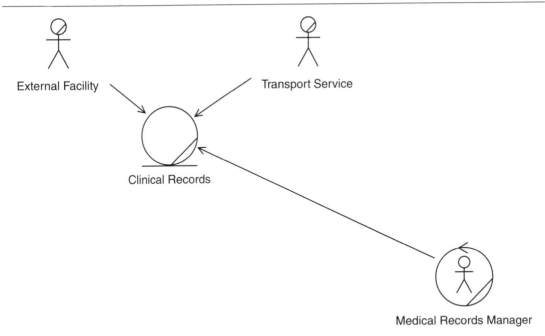

External Facility

Transport Service

Clinical Records

Medical Records Manager

Figure 3–12 Preliminary business object model for the Manage Clinical Records business use case

Facility, the only time the Medical Records Manager just takes the records from the External Facility and stuffs them into the Resident's previous file is when the Resident hasn't been away from the facility long (that is, the records are still open). The Medical Records Manager creates a new file for incoming records of Residents whose files are closed or who are new to the facility. Figure 3–13 shows the flow for Residents entering the Facility.

You see on this diagram two special notes—the rectangles with underlined text and the top right corners turned down. These are not just textual annotations; they are links to two other sequence diagrams. This indicates that, for example, the Admit Prior Resident sequence is performed if needed and then the rest of the Transfer Records In sequence is performed.

We now know there are various types of clinical records. This causes us to update the business object model as shown in Figure 3–14.

The EAB staff indicates the flow is reversed when records are transferred out, so we ask if anything different happens in that case. The business people tell us that they "close" their records on that Resident if the Resident doesn't return within 15 days. No changes can be made when the records are closed. This implies that EAB must keep a schedule for the closure of records.

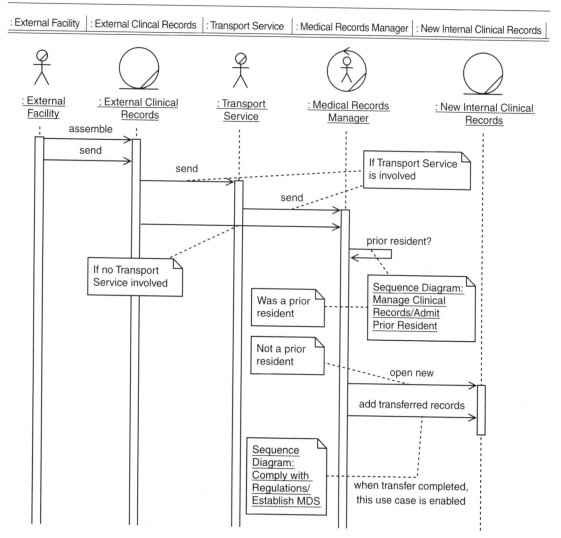

Figure 3–13 Sequence diagram for Transfer Records In

This leads to the question of what happens when the Resident returns after 15 days. In that case, the incoming clinical records are added to a new clinical record file and "linked" to the old (closed) records with a unique identification number. The files are not physically combined. And if the Resident returns before 15 days? The old records are removed from the closure schedule and the incoming records are moved into the existing records (see Figure 3-15).

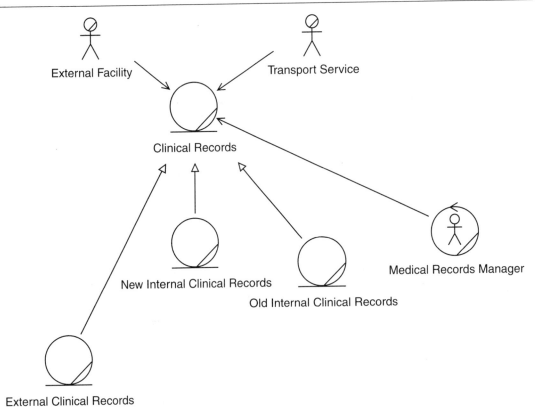

Figure 3–14 Updated business object model for Manage Clinical Records

This diagram shows a link at the beginning to another sequence diagram, Transfer Records In (Figure 3–13). This indicates that the Transfer Records In sequence is performed first and then this sequence, Admit Prior Resident, is performed.

What happens to all the clinical records that are closed or scheduled for closure? The EAB Medical Records Manager tells us that the closure schedule is reviewed regularly, the appropriate records are closed, and then these closed clinical records are archived for seven years. After seven years, the records are destroyed. She also reveals a new piece of information. There is another condition that forces the immediate closure of a Resident's records—when the Resident passes away. This yields the following sequence diagrams, Figures 3–16 and 3–17, and our updated business object model, Figure 3–18.

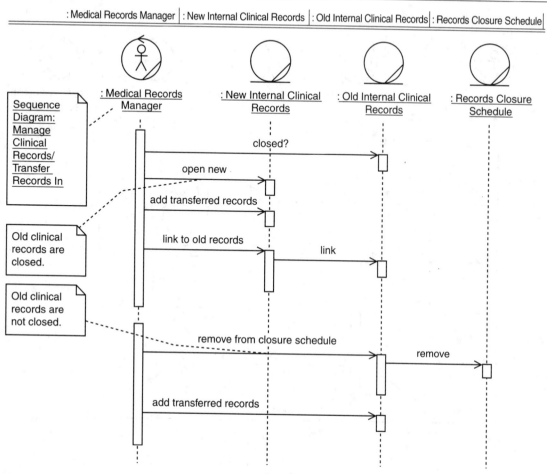

Figure 3–15   Sequence diagram for Admit Prior Resident

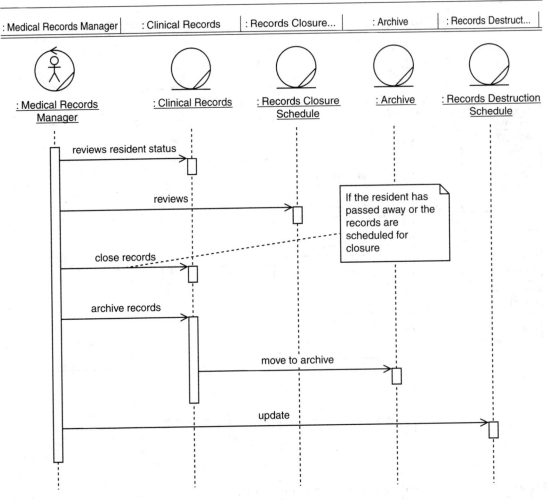

Figure 3–16   Sequence diagram for Close Records

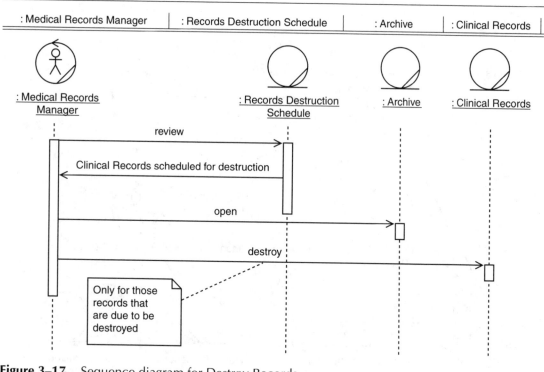

Figure 3–17   Sequence diagram for Destroy Records

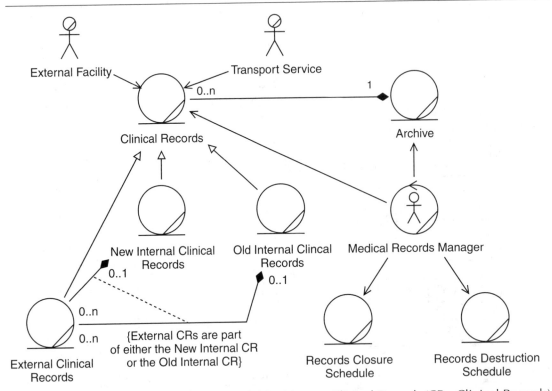

Figure 3–18 Updated business object model for Manage Clinical Records (CRs, Clinical Records)

The External Clinical Records entity in Figure 3–18 is shown as being part of either the New Internal Records or the Old Internal Clinical Records. This constraint is depicted as a dotted line connecting the two composite relationships along with the text description of the constraint in the braces. Some of the relationships also have annotations on the ends that specify multiplicity. The "n" indicates "many," the "0..n" annotation means "zero to many," and exact numbers specify that number as the multiplicity.

This representation of the Clinical Records in the business object model doesn't sit well with Angela, one of the data analysts on the team. The use of *New Internal, Old Internal,* and *External* in the Clinical Records entity names seems to be trying to capture the "state" of these entities. Also, the manner in which the constraint is used seems too easy, possibly masking undiscovered complexities. But since Figure 3–18 does correctly depict the handling of the External Clinical Records and since Angela has no better way in mind to model it, she notes her concern to the team and will wait to see if any further clarification of this comes about during requirements definition or analysis and design.

■ Database Designer

Let's summarize the information that we elicited, just from the Respond to Inquiry and Manage Clinical Records business object models that supports development of the conceptual data model.

New Business Entities

Archive
Records Destruction Schedule
New Internal Clinical Records

Records Closure Schedule
External Clinical Records
Old Internal Clinical Records

New Business Rules

1. Clinical Records are closed after the Resident leaves the Facility for 15 days.
2. Clinical Records are closed when the Resident passes away.
3. Clinical Records are archived after closure.
4. Clinical Records are destroyed after being archived for 7 years.
5. The only time Clinical Records are merged is when the Resident returns within the 15-day closure period. Otherwise, New Internal Clinical Records (incoming) are linked, via a unique identification number, to the Old Internal Clinical Records.
6. The closure and destruction schedules must be checked periodically.

New Access Information

1. The Clinical Records must be accessed by the Facility Staff (read-only) and the Medical Records Manager (read, write, create, destroy, archive).
2. The Medical Records Manager must be able to close (lock) the clinical records.
3. The Facility Staff needs to be able to search through the records. Inquirers do not have direct access to the records.

Considering access, asking about frequency of occurrence of the various actions can give you a head start on performance and sizing considerations. More details in this area will be revealed later in the development cycle as the system definition matures, but any such information known at this point can help with risk assessment and project planning.

Sequence diagrams reveal much of this access and frequency information. Just following the message flow between the entities gives you a direct indication of how heavily these entities, which will likely become tables, will be accessed. Here you can begin to consider your performance issues and gather insight on possible required indexes very early in the development cycle instead of as an afterthought. Also, the sequence diagrams are, in effect, transaction maps that can be used later to validate that your database can support the user's needs.

All of this information is from the two simplest business object models. This is a good return from such a small investment of time. Participating in the business modeling is invaluable to the database designer.

The remaining business use case and business object models can be found in Appendix A. From these you can see the huge amount of information that business modeling gives us. One thing revealed is that many of the business actors and business workers perform many of the same functions. To simplify things these actors can be part of a generalization structure. For example, an Insurance Auditor, Medicare Auditor, Medicaid Auditor, Corporate Auditor, Government Agency, and Administrator are all types of Auditors. Figures 3–19 and 3–20 show the actor generalizations that were revealed as part of the business modeling effort. (Note: Not all the actors are included in these hierarchies.)

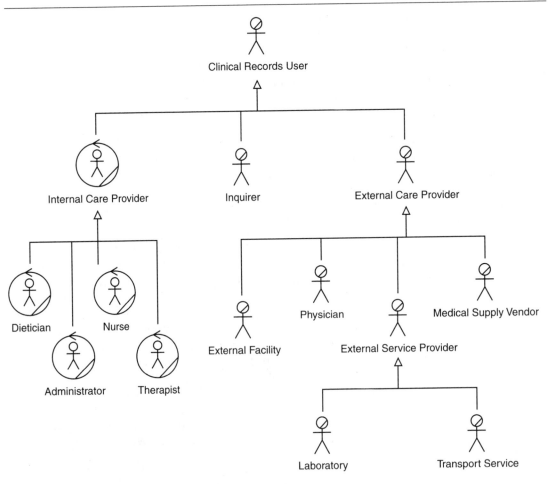

Figure 3–19 Actor generalization for care providers

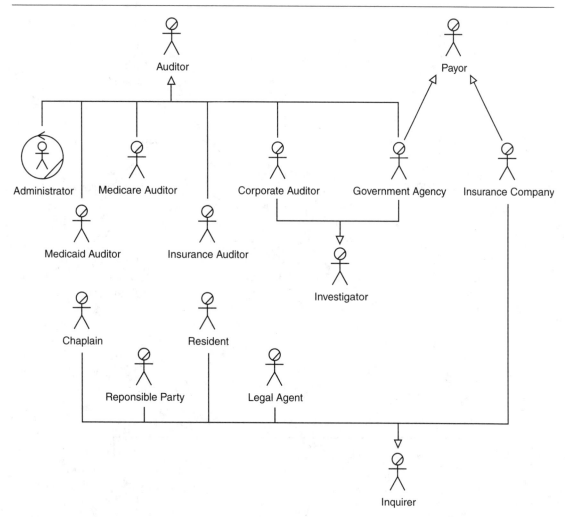

Figure 3–20 Actor generalization for auditors and agents

From all the information revealed during business modeling we can also create a first attempt at a more traditional conceptual data model (Figures 3-21, 3-22, and 3-23). We use the term *traditional* since these models simply show the basic entities, relationships, and some additional high-level information.

While these more traditionally styled data models do express the conceptual data concepts, a conceptual data model comprised of all the diagrams in the business use case and business object models provides a much more robust understanding to the development team.

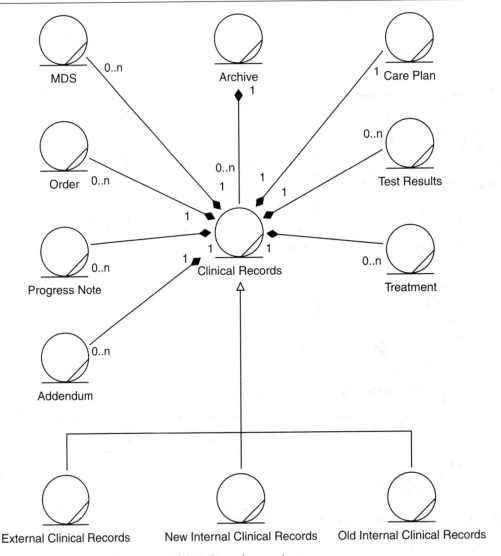

Figure 3–21 Conceptual data model for clinical records

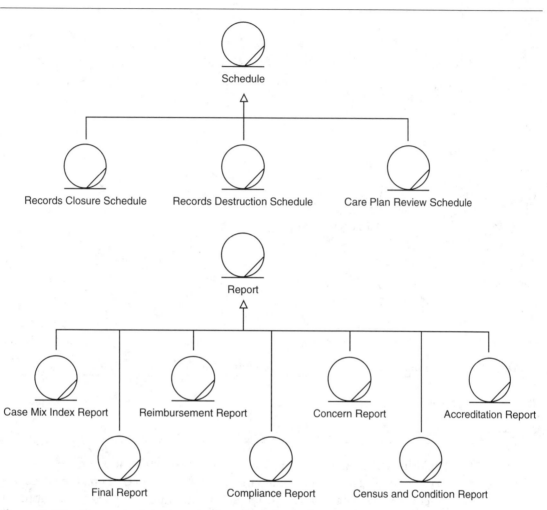

Figure 3–22   Conceptual data model for schedules and reports

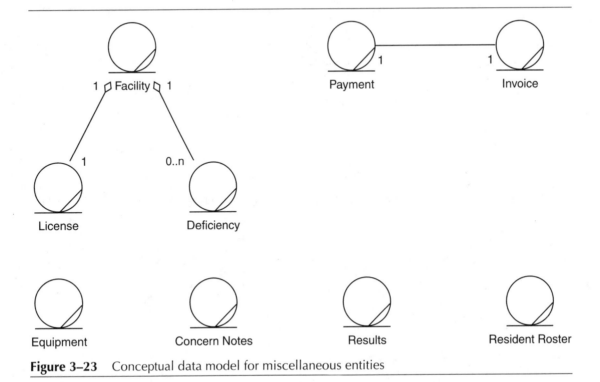

Figure 3–23 Conceptual data model for miscellaneous entities

Summary

Looking at the business use case and business object models, the database designer can begin to understand the data that is needed to build the database. Of course, this data will need elaboration and more will need to be captured, but this gives a good starting point. Using the UML, the teams can share the information gathered and use it in their jobs. The data analyst can share this information and diagrams with the business analysts and developers. (For example, the data analyst can tell them that the attributes of an auditor will probably include a name, address, phone, specialty, and so on and that an auditor may even become a business entity.) The data will be captured in much more detail later, but it is good to get an understanding in the requirements stages rather than just starting with the entity relationship diagrams much later. Use cases also begin the process of uncovering information that will be added to the database. For example, understanding how accounts receivable are handled supplies the data analyst with information about what data need to be captured internally and what data may come from external factors. The more elaborate business models for this case study can be found in Appendix A. We suggest you review them to see just how much information can be obtained from this early work. From a relatively small investment of time, in conjunction with discussions with the business people and a few easy-to-understand diagrams, a database designer can get quite a head start in the development of the system database.

Chapter 4

Requirements Definition

In this chapter we use the abundance of information gathered during the business modeling activities (from Chapter 3 and as shown in Appendix A) to define the system we are building. In this way, we will develop the overall requirements definition of the system to ensure we understand the needs of our "customers"—both internal (the business sponsors responsible for building the system) and external (the end users of the system). This understanding will then be expressed as requirements against which we can plan, build, and test the system.

The Workflow

There are some things that never seem to change, even in the fast-paced world of software development. One of those things is the Iron Triangle. The Iron Triangle is a natural law that pits three forces against each other:

1. The capabilities and quality of the system
2. The development schedule
3. The cost of the development

The Iron Triangle mandates that the magnitude of two of these forces determines the magnitude of the third, or, as it has been heard in uncounted development shops over the years: "Its good, fast, or cheap—pick two!" (In the new

Internet economy the flexibility to "pick two" is often restricted. Commonly, it now must be good and fast from the customer's viewpoint. Unfortunately, from the developer's viewpoint, it may be only fast.)

This simple law of software development makes it imperative that we clearly understand the desired capabilities of the system. This is the one factor (that is, *good*—the capabilities and quality of the system) of the three that we can most easily control. Understanding what we want to build before we begin to build is a major first step toward reducing the risk of failure with our projects. This is why we must clearly define the requirements (that is, the desired capabilities) of the system. We "build to" and test against the requirements. They are our foundation for change and our contract with the business clients. They are not just words on paper. They are critically important.

Our goals for requirements definition are to

1. Establish the scope of the system we are to build
2. Establish a detailed understanding of the desired capabilities of the system

Establishing the scope of the system is often a great personal challenge to the development manager or team leader of the project. This can also be a severe cultural shock to an organization. At this early phase in the development life cycle, our customers (that is, the business people for whom we are building this system) are often like children in a candy store. They want everything. And like those children they never seem to have the money to pay for it all. Unfortunately, those of us on the development side often must play the role of the strict parent, denying our customer's sweet tooth. This can be a career-shortening task if not done properly and gently, which is why we must also meet the second goal of developing a detailed understanding of the desired system capabilities. Indeed, this provides the foundation for achieving the first goal of establishing the system's scope. Bob once worked with a project manager who joined an organization in which the software people often just did whatever they were told by the business clients. This manager came in and through the simple act of prioritizing requirements into "this delivery," "next delivery," "third delivery," and so on he was given the nickname "Dr. No." He caused quite an uproar by simply saying, "No, that will have to go in the next delivery." However, after the cultural trauma abated, he turned out to be one of the most successful project managers that organization ever had.

The Use Case Model

The major artifact that results from requirements definition is the use case model of the system. But didn't we already develop a use case model while modeling the business? Correct, but the use case model to be developed now is the model of the system those business workers and business actors will use to perform their specific business functions. (For those people who don't do business modeling as part of their development process, this is the level of use case modeling at which they typically begin. Also, most texts and articles you may read that discuss use cases typically do so beginning at this level.) Indeed, the elements of the business model (business actors, business workers, business entities, and so on) become part of the system use case model. This gives you a jump start by "preloading" your use case model with these elements.

Supporting the use case model are use case descriptions that elaborate the basic information and detailed flow of the use case. These descriptions should follow a standard format tailored to the organization's needs. There are many examples of use case description templates available in the literature on this topic. However, they should contain, at the minimum:

- Identifying information (name of the use case, who is responsible for the use case, date and/or other revision information)
- A basic description of the use case
- The basic flow of the use case
- Alternate flows and the conditions that trigger them

A more robust description may contain sections on:

- Limitations
- Preconditions (the required state of the system, or conditions that must be true, for the use case to be executed)
- Postconditions (possible states of the system after the execution of the use case)
- Assumptions
- Inclusion and extension points (if using "includes" and "extends" relationships with this use case) and so forth

Examples of such a form appear in Appendix B.

Often, businesses that have an existing system being updated or replaced also have existing documentation on that system, or if they are building a new system, they have used a methodology where technical specifications are written first. This can create confusion when the development team intends to employ use cases also. Questions like "What do we do now?" and "What do we do first—the use cases or the specs?" are asked often. It really doesn't matter. If you have specifications or other supplemental information, they can be a great source for identifying actors, use cases, classes, timing, and other important information. If you have none, building a use case model can help you in building your specifications. Use the information you have to your best advantage and do not allow your progress to be hobbled by excessive devotion to the letter of the law of a specific methodology. Use cases can be used for both capturing existing requirements and eliciting new requirements.

The Case Study Status

The business modeling has been completed for EAB Healthcare. (As we mentioned in the last chapter, in this type of development, which typically takes an iterative approach, you can never assume that something is completed, once and for all, never to change again. Nevertheless, the business modeling is complete enough to proceed to the next major activity.) The business and development teams feel comfortable with their understanding of the way the business operates now and the way the business people want it to operate in the future. The teams were quite surprised with the amount of information that business modeling yielded. Critical timing and numerous other business rules were revealed while the details of the business use cases were elaborated (see various diagrams in Appendix A, such as Figure A–18, the Comply with Regulations /Establish MDS sequence diagram, and Figure A–22, the Maintain MDS sequence diagram, among others). The business team has provided copies of the critical sections of the currently paper-based clinical records that they want automated. These will be used as supplemental specifications to prototype the new user interface and to add details to the data model.

The Concepts

The following UML, object-oriented, and other concepts are cited in this chapter. For a more complete discussion and more rigorous definitions of UML concepts, refer to Booch et al. [1999].

Use case model—typically refers to the use case model of the information system being built versus the business use case model. It is a depiction of how the system capabilities (depicted as use cases) are used by the actors.

"Extends"—a stereotype of a relationship that indicates an optional use case flow that may be executed, based on a specific criterion.

"Includes"—a stereotype of a relationship that indicates a use case flow that is inserted into another use case or use cases at one or more points.

The Approach

In the previous chapter we discussed the benefits gained by the database team being involved in business modeling along with the application development team. Those same benefits are still valid during the development of the system use case model. However, now those same benefits are extended to the developers. Often developers (and database designers) have no knowledge of the business for which they build software systems. Since the information from the business models is used to "preload" the system use case model and other subsequent models, the team members can now begin to understand the business context in which their system is intended to operate.

If you look at the many studies published on the failure of development projects, you will see that, invariably, in the top 10 reasons for failure are two items:

- Misunderstanding the user's needs—this includes the user not participating in the development, the developer ignoring the user's input, vague user needs, and so on.
- Misunderstanding the system requirements—this includes vague, nonexistent, incorrect, missing, and changing requirements.

Being involved in the requirements definition can only help reduce the risk on your development project. Also, errors caught at this early stage of development are much less costly (in both time and money) to fix than those found during system testing.

Involving the Database Team

The venue for much of the requirements definition phase will likely be somewhat different than that for business modeling even though the team will be dealing with many of the same artifacts. Much of the work in this phase is translation and structuring—prime areas for system and data architects. The level of participation by the business people now will typically begin to wane slightly. This is simply because of the nature of the tasks.

Let's look at the "translation" tasks. The abundance of model elements discovered during business modeling must be brought into the system use case model. This is primarily an architectural task, not a business task. The first cut at this process can be very straightforward since many of the same elements just come directly from the business to the use case model. For example, some possible transformations, suggested by the Rational Unified Process, are listed in Table 4–1.

Of course, these are potential initial transformations that can easily change as analysis proceeds. Automating an entire function can eliminate a business

Table 4–1   Business Model to System Use Case Model Transformation

In the Business Model		*In the Use Case Model*
Business use cases	*become*	Subsystems
Business actors	*become*	Actors
Business workers	*become*	Actors or use cases
Business workers' activities	*become*	Use cases

worker; thus, a business worker could become a use case. For example, the function of a typical salesperson (a business worker) in a brick-and-mortar retail store can be Web-enabled. Thus, some of the functions that were performed by that salesperson can be shared between the Online Client (a business actor) and an Online Sale use case. Note that business entities were not forgotten in Table 4–1. They will appear as entity classes, not in the use case model but subsequently in the analysis and/or design models.

Once these initial translations are made, the business people play a very important role as validators and elaborators. When the architects decided to automate that business worker in the previous example, was the manner in which that split was done consistent with how the business people want the business to operate? The business people must validate these types of functional adaptations that the development team chooses to make. Also, definition of additional system use cases needed to realize the business model must be done with the agreement of the business people. At this point, regular sessions with the business people will prove valuable since they will be able to elaborate the interactions between the system use cases and the actors.

One effective way to utilize the business people during this period is to familiarize them with the use case description templates you will use to elabo-

■ **Database Designer**

As these transformations occur and new actors and use cases are created, remember that, just as in the business modeling phase, these likely will become entities (for example, actors) in your data model or will generate additional entities (as new use case descriptions and/or sequence diagrams are updated or newly created). This will allow you to further refine your conceptual data model.

rate the detailed flow of the use case. Once comfortable with the format, there is nobody who can better elaborate what the use cases should do than the business people. Often we have found that, given a little mentoring on use case development and the templates, the business folks are willing to define the flows of the use cases. This increases the quality of the use case definitions and helps avoid the introduction of "translation" errors, which can occur if the development team defines the use cases on its own.

One warning: be very careful when developing the use case model. If you use the "extends" or "includes" stereotypes in your modeling, avoid falling into functional decomposition. Use cases are not comprised of multiple lower-level use cases. A business use case may be "realized" by numerous system use cases, but it does not decompose into these system use cases, nor should the system use cases be decomposed into smaller use cases. Remember, *each* use case is a *complete* flow of events that produces a result of *value* to the actor. If you decompose a use case you break the "completeness" of the use case. For example, if you have a use case, Withdraw Cash, for an automatic teller machine, this use case *does not* decompose into Insert Card, Enter PIN, Select Account, and similar use cases. Each of these individually is not a complete flow nor does each individually provide value to the actor.

■ Database Designer

What may be the most valuable aspect of requirements definition and its use case modeling for the database designer is ensuring correct concepts. Most companies do not throw away their databases. However, applications are regularly significantly modified or even discarded. What is the probability that the newly hired developer on your project will correctly understand the context and structure of your existing database's Account table? Can it really be accessed by that attribute/column? Does it even have that column? Or will she just make the assumption that accounts are accounts and proceed to use the account abstraction as she sees fit in the system design? If you don't find this out early in the development, how much "damage" will this cause later to your database design when you have to make a last-minute change to the database to fix this misunderstanding? Everyone must understand and agree to these critical definitions before significant time and effort are expended to solidify possibly erroneous concepts deep in the application design. The database designer is in a key position to ensure these critical concepts are correctly captured and understood.

Table 4–2 Business Use Case Prioritization

Business Use Case	*Priority*	*Which Delivery/Iteration*
Comply with Regulations	High	First
Manage Clinical Records	High	First
Provide Clinical Care	High	First
Respond to Inquiry	Med	Second
Accounts Receivable	Low	Second

The Design

The business model that was developed for EAB Healthcare raised considerable concern with the development team. All of the various flows that were captured showing how the facility's external interfaces interacted with the facility's people and systems caused the specter of scope creep to haunt them. Fortunately, as mentioned earlier, through the close cooperation with the business people, the desire is to focus only on the parts of the business that use the clinical records. From the vision statement of the project, one of the major goals is to improve staff efficiency by reducing the volumes of paperwork that must be handled. The intent is to make EAB Healthcare a more efficient business.

Therefore, with this guidance in hand, the team begins to limit the scope of the effort. There is no need to model all the activities of the business actors when they are not interacting with the system. The business modeling also showed many reports are created as a result of numerous processes. However, these records are not handled with high frequency by many people and thus can be deferred to a later delivery. With these insights the development team now concentrates on keeping the scope of the project focused on the medical records that are constantly used, every day, by most of the staff. This focus motivated the developers to name the new system "OMaR" for the **O**nline **M**edical **R**ecords system.

This drives the team to conclude that the Accounts Receivable and Respond to Inquiry business use cases should be deferred to a later delivery. This allows the development effort to focus on the business use cases with higher value: Comply with Regulations, Manage Clinical Records, and Provide Clinical Care (Table 4-2).

Moving from the Business Model to the System Model

Unfortunately for the members of the development team, they do not have the advantage of having textual specifications for the system they are to build. They are working in an industry (elder care) that does not traditionally embrace such discipline and typically does not have the budget to develop such specifications. So OMaR's requirements will be elicited using a use case approach. The resulting requirements will take the form of use cases, use case models, and whatever supplemental documents the team can obtain.

Beginning with the Comply with Regulations business use case, the team starts the transition to the system use case model. Looking at the business use case model Provide Resident Care (see Figure 3-6), you can see the three business actors Data Broker, Government Agency, and Corporate Auditor interact with the Comply with Regulations use case and must be brought into the system use case model. However, the Government Agency and Corporate Auditor were generalized as an Investigator business actor (see Figure 3-20). So initially, the Investigator and the Data Broker will be included in the system use case model.

In the original activity diagrams for Comply with Regulations two business actors are cited: the Medical Records Manager and the Government Agency. In dealing with compliance, most of the interaction with the Government Agency really falls to the Nurses and the Administrator of the facility. Therefore, these two business workers will appear in the system use case model instead of the more generic Facility Staff. Also, since the Government Agency is only one type of Investigator, the more general Investigator actor will be used here (see Figures 4-1a and 4-1b).

The only function of the Medical Records Manager in this scenario is to provide access to the records. This is where the development team begins the process of automating the functions of the Medical Records Manager. Thus, the Medical Records Manager will not move into the system use case model, but the activity performed, providing access to the clinical records, will appear as a new use case, Access Clinical Records. Further examination of the activity diagrams for this business use case shows many other activities, but they are operational activities that the external actors perform manually (for example, Interview Staff, Inspect Facility). Therefore, no other activity will be brought over to the system use case diagram. This leads to the simple use case diagram shown in Figure 4-2.

Turning to the business object model for Comply with Regulations (Figure 4-3) we see many different entities here. Before just bringing them into the system use case model, let's remember the focus of this development—medical records that are constantly used, every day, by most of the staff. Examining the various sequence diagrams for this model (see Appendix A, Figures A-17 through A-24), the team concludes that the sequences for Review Compliance, Accreditation, and Investigate Concerns mostly fall into three categories: operational activities, completely external activities, and activities that do not require any significant Clinical Records support (many of the report entities are not

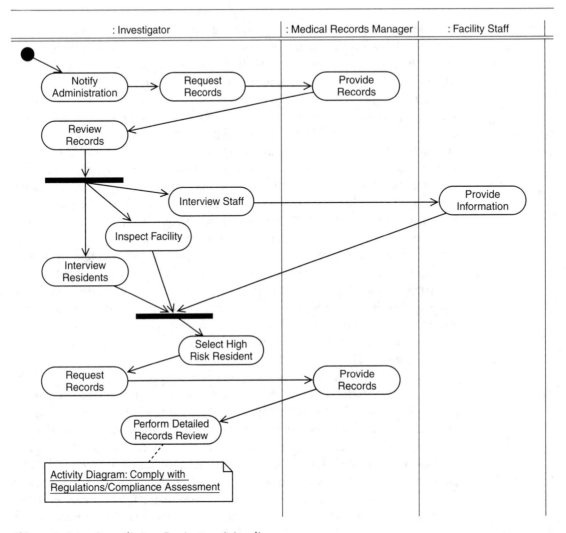

Figure 4–1a Compliance Review activity diagram

part of the Clinical Records). Therefore, these will be scoped out to a future delivery (Table 4–3).

Why look at the sequence diagrams for this scope and prioritization exercise? The activities depicted in these sequences are eventually going to find their way into one or more system use cases (possibly as main flows, alternate flows, error conditions, and so on), as discussed previously. Rather than wait for all the use cases to be fully defined and elaborated, we can do an early assessment. Thus, we avoid doing all that work to define things we are not going to develop.

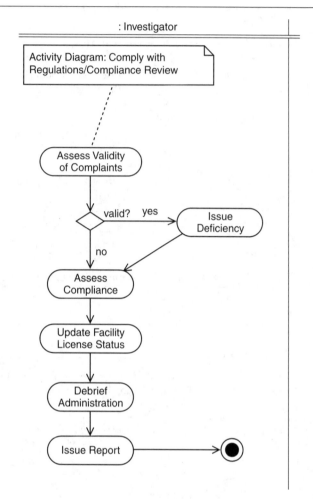

Figure 4–1b Compliance Assessment activity diagram

This leaves the three sequences to Establish, Maintain, and Transmit the Minimum Data Sets (MDSs). These fit the criteria for the current focus of the project very well since the MDSs are the centerpiece documents around which compliance revolves. Examining these sequences leads us to bring these key activities, performed by the business workers, into the system use case diagrams as new use cases: Establish MDS, Maintain MDS, and Transmit MDS (Figure 4-4).

Now the team continues along the same line with the other business use cases: Manage Clinical Records and Provide Clinical Care. Manage Clinical Records is absolutely central to the functioning of the system. Therefore, all the

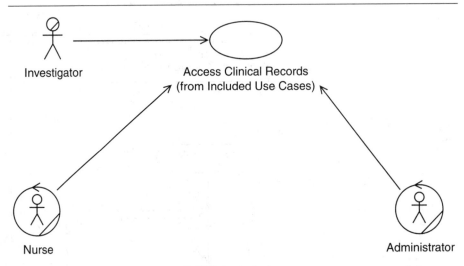

Figure 4–2   Preliminary Comply with Regulations system use case model

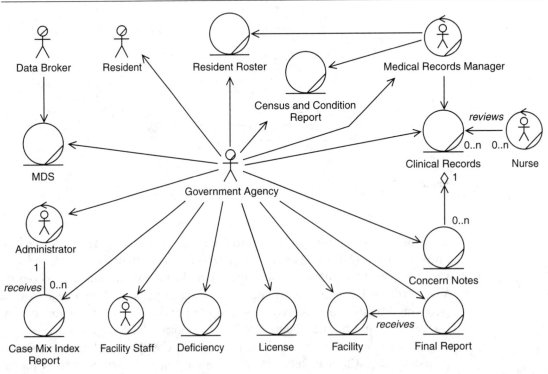

Figure 4–3   Comply with Regulations business object model

Table 4–3 Comply with Regulations Business Object Model Sequence Prioritization

Sequence	Priority	Which Delivery/ Iteration	Rationale
Establish MDS	High	First	Critical
Maintain MDS	High	First	Critical
Transmit MDS	High	First	Critical
Investigate Concerns	Medium	Second	Mostly external/minimal support needed
Review Compliance	Low	Second	Minimal support needed
Accreditation	None	None	Fully external

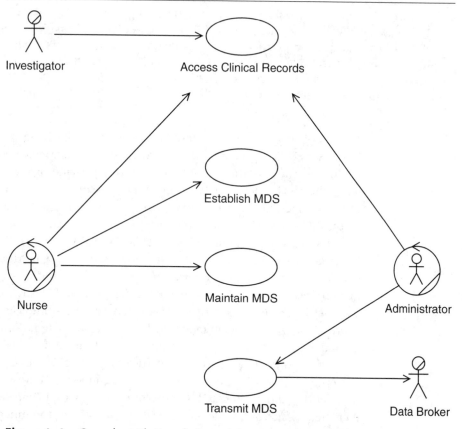

Figure 4–4 Comply with Regulations system use case model

■ **Database Designer**

The database designer should take note of the significant business rules that are expressed in the sequence diagrams that have to do with MDS processing:

1. The first MDS must be established by the Assessment Reference Date.
2. The Assessment Reference Date = 5 days after admission for Medicare patients.
3. The Assessment Reference Date = 14 days after admission for non-Medicare patients.
4. A new MDS must be created for Medicare patients 5, 14, 30, 60, and 90 days after admission.
5. MDSs must be updated quarterly.
6. MDSs must be updated annually.
7. MDSs must be updated when a patient's condition shows a significant change.
8. MDSs are transmitted monthly.

These are critical aspects of a key part of the Clinical Records that require special attention due to the volume and frequency of access such business rules imply. This allows you to start planning performance considerations into your system early.

Also, the "winnowing out" process that the team is going through to prioritize and control the scope of the project allows you to focus on the critical business entities (for example, MDS, Clinical Records) and establish a solid core database. These are the use cases that must be paid great attention. You can leave the less critical data (for example, Case Mix Index Report) for subsequent deliveries.

aspects of this business use case will be included in the current delivery. This business use case primarily defines the functions the Medical Records Manager performs. The other actors involved merely provide or receive information. Since the Medical Records Manager's functions are targets for automation, many of these functions become "reassigned" to new use cases, new actors, and the Medical Records Manager. Simple ones such as the transfer of records manifest in the system use case model as Access Clinical Records and Update Clinical Records use cases. More complex functions, such as the management of the closure and destruction of records, according to the business rules specified, become Manage Records, Close Clinical Records, and Destroy Clinical Records use cases. The development team also has created some use cases that were overlooked in the business modeling but became apparent during requirements definition (Create Clinical Records, Unarchive Clinical Records, and Verify Security Permission). The resulting system use case model is shown in Figure 4-5.

A new actor (Clinical Records User) was added to represent all the various users of the Clinical Records. A more interesting actor (Time) was added to depict the passage of time, which is critical to some of the functions performed (for example, Manage Records).

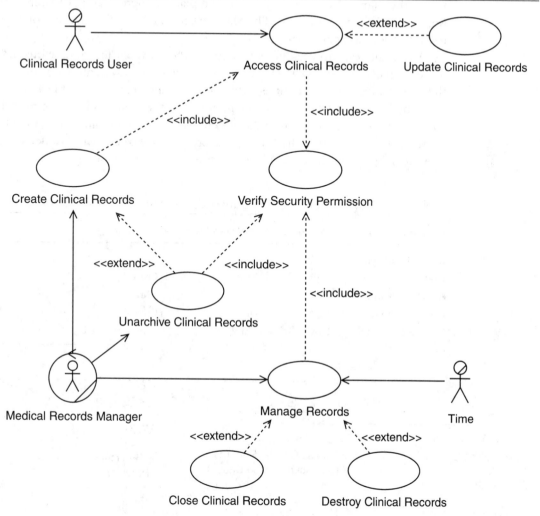

Figure 4–5 Manage Clinical Records system use case model

The team notes an interesting outcome of this analysis. The Manage Clinical Records use case (Figure 4-5) can also fulfill the needs expressed in the Respond to Inquiry business use case (Figure 3-10). The only part of Respond to Inquiry that needs system support is the access to the Clinical Records. (The role played by the Facility Staff will be fully automated in the new system.) As can be seen in Figure 4-5, access is provided via the Clinical Records User actor. We merely have to add the Inquirer to the Clinical Records User hierarchy. (This change also simplifies the Provide Clinical Care use case diagram, in which the Clinical Records User can now replace numerous actors.) Therefore, Respond to Inquiry is subsumed by Manage Clinical Records and does not need to be developed separately.

When the team applies the new focus on the Provide Clinical Care business use case, most of it survives. This business use case already centers on some of the most critical business entities—the Care Plan and Treatment (Table 4-4).

When the team brings model elements from the business use case models and business object models into the system use case model, eliminating the elements that are not part of the Clinical Records or are external to EAB (deferring these to subsequent deliveries), the results are shown in Figure 4-6.

Table 4–4 Provide Clinical Care Business Object Model Sequence Prioritization

Sequence	Priority	Which Delivery	Rationale
Establish Care Plan	High	First	Critical
Update Care Plan	High	First	Critical
Establish Treatment	High	First	Critical
Update Treatment	High	First	Critical
Provide Services	Low	Third	Mostly external

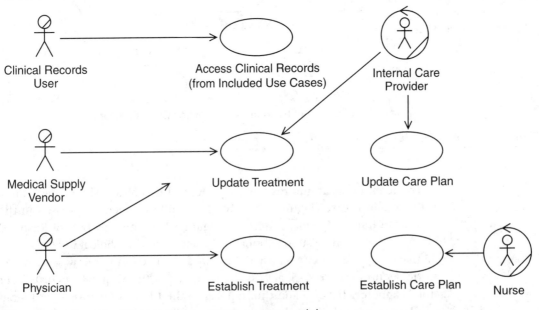

Figure 4–6 Provide Clinical Care system use case model

■ Database Designer

Consider what has been accomplished during the business modeling and requirements definitions phases to this point. The team has defined various actors. Most of these actors represent the roles people perform. The specification of roles is important for the database designer when security is considered. While this is usually a consideration during physical database design, since we are using the UML, these roles (and the entities they access) are defined much earlier in the life cycle.

In fact, once the team develops the business and system use case models, what have really been defined are the various "user views" Also, since these business model elements migrate into the system use case model, what is actually happening is the integration of all the user views into one common conceptual view. This integrated view is an extremely valuable result of the development process, especially when these models are developed in conjunction with the application developers. This not only provides the database designer an excellent foundation upon which to develop a quality database but it also gives everyone on the team a shared understanding. This common understanding between application and database developers usually never materializes during more traditional development processes.

Proceeding in this fashion (that is, merging the business models into the system models) using the UML also gives the database designer a relatively straightforward way to proceed in these early phases and yields valuable results. Typical guidance given for gathering the user's requirements often is very simplistic—talk to the users or watch what the users do on the job or send out questionnaires and job surveys and so on. Then what? Often the designer is left to just shuffle all this raw information together in some form. Using the UML as has been done here gives you a simple, standard way to proceed and represent this important information.

This is a surprisingly simple use case diagram. This is because actors that are higher up in the actor hierarchy represent many of the actors (for example, External Care Provider, Internal Care Provider) and most of the activities (use cases) performed by the actors are simply accessing and updating the records. The actual medical treatments are operational activities that make up much of what these actors do. However, it is only the results of the operational activities that are captured by OMaR.

You may note in Figure 4-6 that one of the use cases is annotated "(from Included Use Cases)." This merely indicates that we have put some use cases into their own package (Included Use Cases) because they are included in many different use case diagrams.

Inside the System Use Cases

Each of the system use cases must be elaborated in further detail. This can be done with a relatively simple use case template (Figure 4-7).

Use Case Description

Use Case Name:
Use Case Purpose:

Point of Contact:
Date Modified:

Preconditions:
Postconditions:

Limitations:
Assumptions:

Basic Flow:
    A.
    B.
    C.
    and so on

Alternate Flow:
    Condition Triggering Alternate Flow:
    B1.
    B2.
    B3.
    and so on

Figure 4–7 Basic use case description template

There are many different variations on this type of template. Tailor it to your own needs, but don't make it so formal as to make it cumbersome to use. Most of the fields in the sample use case template are self-explanatory. Keep the use case purpose brief—three to five sentences. Preconditions are conditions that must be true for the use case to execute. Postconditions are important conditions that are true after the use case basic flow is executed. The basic flow elaborates the steps followed in a successful execution of the use case. These steps can also indicate where "extended" or "included" use cases are executed. The alternate flows elaborate alternate paths that are followed when the triggering condition is true. These alternate flows augment the basic flow. For example, when the triggering condition occurs, the basic flow of the use case changes from steps A, B, C, and so on to steps A, B, B1, B2, B3, B4, C, and so on. An example can be seen in Figure 4-8.

Each system use case should have its own use case description. But as we've warned before, beware of analysis paralysis—the condition where you attempt to analyze every possible part and variant of the system and thus never complete the analysis and move forward in the project. There are probably a nearly infinite number of conditions that could trigger an alternate flow. So how many do you examine? We can confidently give the definitive answer—it

Use Case Description—OMaR Project

Use Case Name: **Access Clinical Records**

Use Case Purpose: The purpose of this use case is to allow the Clinical Records information to be accessed by the appropriate actors.

Point of Contact:

Date Modified:

Preconditions: None identified.

Postconditions: Clinical Records will be unlocked after being accessed by the Clinical Records User. They will remain locked until the Clinical Records User updates or "returns" the Clinical Records.

Limitations: Only the same Clinical Records User to whom the Clinical Records were released can provide updates or return the Clinical Records.

Assumptions: None identified.

Basic Flow:

- A.   The Clinical Records User identifies herself or himself to OMaR.
- B.   INCLUSION: Perform Verify Security Permission Use Case. OMaR verifies the Clinical Records User's security access, permissions, etc.
- C.   The Clinical Records User specifies the Clinical Record by Resident.
- D.   The Clinical Record is made available for the Clinical Records User to view.
- E.   If the Clinical Records User wants to update the Clinical Record, EXTENSION: Perform Update Clinical Record use case.
- F.   If Resident is being transferred out of the facility, update Records Closure Schedule and create a copy of the Clinical Record for the Clinical Records User.
- G.   If the Clinical Records User wants to access additional records, go to step C.

Alternate Flow:

Condition Triggering Alternate Flow: OMaR does not recognize the Clinical Records User as having access to the system.

- B1.   If verification of the Clinical Records User's identification has failed three times, OMaR will disable this data entry interface. OMaR logs these attempts in the security log. This use case then terminates.
- B2.   If verification of the Clinical Records User's identification has not yet failed three times, OMaR asks the Clinical Records User to re-enter identification.
- B3.   OMaR repeats step B in the Basic Flow.

Condition Triggering Alternate Flow: OMaR does not recognize the Clinical Records User as having permission to review the Clinical Records.

- C1.   Access to the Clinical Records is denied.
- C2.   OMaR tells the Clinical Records User that he or she does not have sufficient permission to review the Clinical Records.
- C3.   OMaR returns to step A in the Basic Flow.

Figure 4–8   Completed use case description template for Access Clinical Records

depends. It depends on many factors, such as the criticality of the use case, the level of domain knowledge of the development staff, and whether the software run attended or unattended, local or remote. Is it a real-time system with failure conditions that are catastrophic or trivial? You could go on for days defining every alternate path for every minute error condition, but that is not the intent.

For candidate conditions that could trigger alternate paths, some items to consider include

- Interfaces. What if an interface to/from another part of the system does not provide what is needed for this use case?
- Time. What if things happen sooner or later than expected?
- Hardware. What if a key component fails? What if its backup fails?
- Critical processing. What if the security capabilities fail?
- Availability. What if data, hardware, or some other critical item is not available to the use case?

Does this mean you should have alternate paths for each of these? No. If they are important to your system, add them. Leave the trivial error processing for the developers to handle. As a final test, ask yourself, "Do I really understand the behavior of this use case?"

At this point in the case study, the development team realizes they still need a great deal of business user input to fully develop the use case descriptions. Also, since the business users are going to have to approve the descriptions anyway, the team decides to invest in a bit of use case training for the business folks. They hold a two-day workshop where everyone learns the basic use case symbols (not the entire UML), the proper use of the use case description template, and a few exercises. At the end of this workshop, the business people can write a use case description as well as the developers. Since the business people know their business and know what they want better than the development team does, the group decides that the business people will write the use case descriptions. This is more efficient since it eliminates "translation" errors by the development team and eliminates additional unneeded review and correction cycles. See Appendix B for OMaR's use case descriptions.

There is one caveat when pursuing this direction. Some of the business folks may really get the hang of modeling and may become very "confident" in their abilities. As you proceed further into analysis and design you must enforce the rule that only the designers model. Business people direct *what* the system must do, focusing on the business level flows of control and data (stopping at the system boundary). The designers and implementers determine *how* these capabilities are modeled and implemented, respectively. Allow this rule to be broken and you risk your system due to models that may be semantically incorrect.

Summary

So, where are we? Let's look back to where we've been. During business modeling we selected five business use cases and defined their respective business object models: Accounts Receivable, Comply with Regulations, Manage Clinical Records, Provide Clinical Care, and Respond to Inquiry. During that phase, the high-level activity diagrams for the business use cases drove multiple and more detailed sequence diagrams in the business object model. For example, for the Manage Clinical Records business use case, the activity Transfer Records To/From Facility spawned five sequence diagrams in the business object model, depicting the internal business activities: Transfer Records In, Transfer Records Out, Close Records, Destroy Records, and Admit Prior Resident.

With the business model sufficiently elaborated, we moved into requirements definition. Before proceeding, the development team performed some scope reduction. They deferred the Accounts Receivable and Respond to Inquiry business use cases, in total, to later deliveries. The Comply with Regulations and Provide Clinical Care business use cases were partially descoped, focusing them on the critical internal information and goals of the project. The Manage Clinical Records use case was not descoped due to the central role it plays in the system. However, it was significantly restructured in the system use case model (see Table 4–5). Such changes are not abnormal and should be expected as the system evolves. Also, two use cases evolved as being central to all the various use case models: Access Clinical Records and Verify Security Permission. With the requirements captured in the business use case model, the business object model, the system use case model (including their respective activity and sequence diagrams), and the system use case descriptions, the team is ready to proceed with analysis and design.

Table 4–5 Business Model Sequences versus System Use Case Model for Manage Clinical Records

Sequence	System Use Cases	Rationale
Close Records	Close Clinical Records	
Destroy Records	Destroy Clinical Records	
Admit Prior Resident	Manage Clinical Records	The original three sequences were restructured
Transfer Records In	Update Clinical Records	into these three new and existing system use cases.
Transfer Records Out	Close Clinical Records	
—	Create Clinical Records	New
—	Unarchive Clinical Records	New

Chapter 5
Analysis and Preliminary Design

In this chapter we transition from the realm of business needs and requirements into the world of designing an information system. At this point, from the use case perspective, we should have a good understanding of what needs to be built. We now proceed with the logical design of the system that will provide the common blueprint for *what* we will build. *How* the system will be built (specific technologies, languages, and so on) comes later in the life cycle.

The Workflow

We are sure that a few of our readers will now give a mental sigh and say, "Finally, we're getting to the good part—building the system. All that other stuff is fluff." We do understand that many people feel that way. After all, what we focus on shapes our perceptions. When a mail carrier is delivering the mail, he is "working." When a carpenter is driving those nails, she is "working." When a system architect is designing a system, he is "working." When a coder is coding, she is "working." So any activity that falls outside their "work" is, by default, "not working" and therefore is perceived to be not valuable or important. Given that these people chose the area in which they wanted to work, not only are these other activities "not work," they are also perceived as not interesting. Not valuable, not work, not important, not interesting equals not needed.

Not so! You see, you will do all of these activities eventually. You must. It's all part of understanding what the problem is and what you need to do. For example, Bob recalls numerous times when he was working as a programmer when he would stop and think, "What should the system do in this case?" If he hadn't been given requirements that specified what to do, he'd think it over, come up with a solution, and continue coding. The system designer hadn't done his job. He hadn't given Bob complete requirements, so Bob had to do the designer's job in addition to his own. If you think that bypassing the preliminary work in favor of a "Ready. Set. Code!" approach will save you time, you are fooling yourself. You will do this work anyway. It will merely be hidden in with the work for which you are primarily responsible. In other words, your predecessors in the software life cycle have shifted their workload onto your back—and they probably didn't give you more time and personnel to handle the extra load. Could this be why the coding phase traditionally consumes the largest amount of time and effort versus any other phase of the software life cycle?

Also, for every ad hoc solution a coder creates because of poor requirements and for every ad hoc solution a system architect creates because of poor understanding of the business user needs, an opportunity is created for more defects to be introduced into the system. Not because the developers are bad but merely because the solution they choose may not be the solution that was desired.

Our goals in analysis and preliminary design are to

1. Establish a system design that will be able to meet the expressed business needs and requirements
2. Establish a common blueprint for all members of the development team

One caveat—we are not going to get into the often heated argument over analysis versus design. Whether you wish to perform analysis and then perform design, or intermix them, or go straight to design, we will leave that choice to you without prejudice. Your development culture, process (if any), project characteristics, and business needs will likely be significant drivers for your decision in this area.

The Class Diagram

The major artifact that results from this activity will be the class diagrams of the system. The class diagram, which shows the static structure of the system, has always been a key, if not the central, diagram in many UML or object-oriented methodologies. But now, with the advent of using the UML for database design, the class diagram becomes even more important. The class diagram now becomes the common, centerpiece diagram that both the application and database developers will use as the foundation for their designs.

Not only does the class diagram establish the main entities in the system and their relationships with each other but it now also does this for both application and database entities. As both groups work together to establish the system design, the database designers will be able to provide the details needed for the persistent classes in the system, rather than the application designers assuming what data is available. This item is particularly challenging as turnover in personnel affects your projects. Does that new Web developer you hired two weeks ago really understand the Accounts table that exists in your legacy database? Does she understand that you even *have* a legacy Accounts table?

The often-contentious area of "business rules" can now be brought into the open via this common model. What implements the business rules—the applications, separate business logic, or the database? With this shared diagram both application and database developers can see, understand, and establish whose responsibility it is to implement a given rule. With both groups working with the same design, these critical rules can be implemented in the most appropriate, nonconflicting manner.

Having this common blueprint and having a common language (that is, the UML) also facilitates change management. There will come a point when the logical model, represented in class diagrams, is sufficiently developed and then the two teams will separate to complete their respective designs (application and database). Application designers will continue to develop the common class diagrams to sufficient detail that the application can be coded (exactly where the cutover to coding happens is particular to the organization, culture, staff skill level, and so on). The database designers will take the common diagram, once most of the attributes are sufficiently established, and transform it into a data model. They will then continue with their detailed design using this data model. When changes occur (whether driven by the business, the application design, the database design, or other project aspects) the impact can be established on the common class model and then rippled down into both the detailed application and database models more simply since they all use one language. (The UML, as a notation alone, will not be sufficient for systems of any substantial size. A configuration-management system and a change-management system will also be required.)

Not only is there an advantage to using the models to track changes while moving forward but using the same base artifacts from the early requirements through to the analysis phases also helps to ensure that the different teams are using the same information as they move forward. When starting in different environments or not even beginning with a combined requirements phase, it is very likely that you will end up with multiple entities with the same definition or similar entities with very different definitions.

Supporting Diagrams and Activities

The class diagrams will not stand alone. There should be sequence diagrams to establish or support the class diagrams. These may be new sequences or old sequences that need to be further elaborated. Looking back, the use cases or sequence diagrams that seemed to be sufficient for business modeling or requirements definition may be of insufficient detail for analysis and design. Even they may be revisited and refined. (Not to worry since this is an iterative development cycle.) Also, for more complex behavior, statechart diagrams, activity diagrams, and others may be needed.

The Case Study Status

Eager to begin the design phase, the EAB Healthcare development team, using its prioritization plan, starts with the design of the high-priority use cases for the Comply with Regulations business use case: Establish Minimum Data Set (MDS), Maintain MDS, and Transmit MDS. Recall that these are key since the MDSs are the centerpiece documents around which compliance revolves. However, we will see that in their haste to "get it done," the team members' previous lightweight treatment of certain areas will come back to haunt them.

The Concepts

The following UML, object-oriented, and other concepts are cited in this chapter. For a more complete discussion and more rigorous definitions of UML concepts, refer to Booch et al. [1999].

Statechart—a diagram that shows the dynamic behavior of a class

Control class—an active class that controls the behavior of one or more other classes

Passive class—a class that is not active and does not embody any control of the system

The Approach

Typically, the approach at this point in the development cycle is straightforward. Similar to the business-level modeling, for each of the system use cases a textual flow of events should be developed (in much more detail than what was done in use case development), followed by a sequence diagram. From these a class diagram will be developed. But how do you go from the use cases and sequence diagrams to a class diagram? Development approaches that start at the system level (that is, no business modeling) usually have very general guidelines to "discover" the candidate classes for the class diagram. While these guidelines can work and are simple to understand (for example, "Pick out all the nouns in the problem statement and make them the candidate classes") it often produces a class model that poses many questions, especially for the developers who are new to this type of approach.

However, having done the earlier business-level work, the EAB team will have an advantage. Previously we saw how the information from the business models can be used to "preload" the system use case model, thus giving that model's development a jump start. Now we will see the same effect as information from the system use case model is used to jump-start the development of the class diagrams of the system. For example, since we used sequence diagrams to elaborate the business object model, these can be brought forward to provide a framework for more detailed sequence diagrams for the system model.

Involving the Database Team

Similarly, concepts used by the database developers can be used to jump-start your class model. Many database developers work with the concept of user views. These views basically depict how the various users access the data to accomplish the task at hand. Indeed, one could argue that a user view is a simpler form of a business object model.

■ **Database Designer**

As the sequence diagrams are updated or newly created, ensure that they are elaborated well because they too may serve a dual purpose. Once your database design is created, the sequence diagrams can be used to validate your database design to ensure that the database can support the needs of the users. After all, the sequence diagrams are a good depiction of the data used, in what sequence, by the users as they execute a "transaction" with the system. During detailed database design, tables may be merged, split, or deleted. Does the data the users need still exist and can they get access to it? The sequence diagrams can help you validate the database before you go "live." Sequence diagrams also help you begin to understand the need for indexes. By understanding how the communication among objects occurs, and eventually among tables through sequence diagrams, you get a preview of what columns are accessed and how often and where indexes may be suitable.

Why not build the user views from the existing business models we have developed and use them as the start of the class model? Such initial class models will have only passive classes in them, but that is all right since they are serving only as a framework upon which to build—another jump start. An additional advantage to this approach, if you are using visual modeling tools to automate your design process, is that all of the relationships among these elements being brought forward will be maintained and the integrity of the design will remain intact.

The Design

You Want to Do What?!

After requirements definition, Angela, one of the data analysts on the team, approached Mike, the system's architect, and reasserted her previous concerns about the business object model for Manage Clinical Records. (Mike understood that such an apparent "back step" is not uncommon during an object-oriented development process and indeed is usually very valuable. Problems avoided increase quality and speed development. He also understood that this would be a hard sell to project management.) As you recall, during business modeling, Angela expressed concern about how the Clinical Records were being modeled (see Figure 3-18). The use of *New, Old,* and *External* in the Clinical Records entity names seemed to be trying to capture the "state" of these entities or possibly trying to capture time-variant behavior of the various Clinical Records entities. The understanding that she developed while working through requirements definition only increased her concern. After reviewing it together Mike agreed, and they set about to remodel that business object model.

Their first rework is shown in Figures 5-1 and 5-2. They simplified the model by splitting it into two diagrams. The first, Figure 5-1, captures just the relationships of other elements to the Clinical Records (CR). The second, Figure 5-2, captures the relationships among the types of Clinical Records. It is here where Angela's concerns lie.

They felt that Figure 5-2 more clearly expressed the relationships among the types of Clinical Records. However, there still seemed to be some implicit time or state behavior in these relationships. So they went back to the business people and asked if this model properly described the situation. The business folks verified that the model did correctly describe the handling of External Clinical Records. (External Clinical Records simply become part of the Old Clinical Records if the Old Clinical Records are open. If the Old Clinical Records are closed, the External Clinical Records are put into a New Clinical Record that is linked to the old, closed ones.) However, they also revealed that in

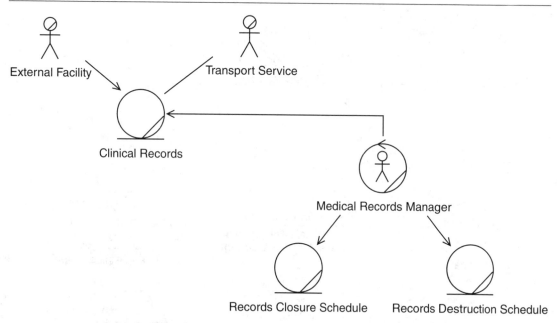

Figure 5–1 Modified business object model for Manage Clinical Records (Part 1)

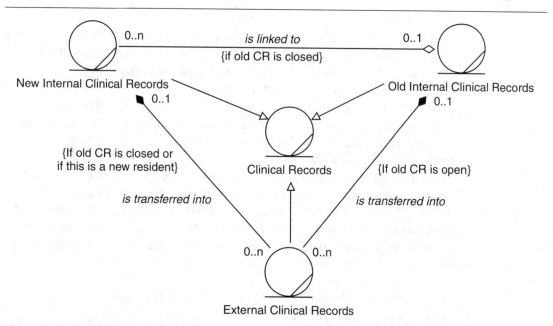

Figure 5–2 Modified business object model for Manage Clinical Records (Part 2)

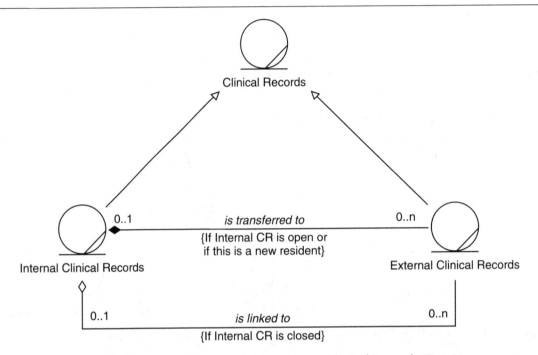

Figure 5–3 Simplified business object model for Manage Clinical Records (Part 2)

the business they do not really have New Clinical Records. The business people think of them as only Internal Clinical Records and External Clinical Records. This led the development team to the model shown in Figure 5-3.

While simpler, this model still has the same shortcomings of the previous models; the state of the files is bound up in the constraints on the relationships. The team also realizes that these depictions focus on what to do with the External Clinical Records only. What about the possibility of linking multiple sets of Internal Clinical Records? Is that a valid situation?

Angela suggested that they try modeling the Clinical Records with the concept of "state" (that is, open records, closed records, and so on) separate from the rest of the model. The team members also decided to test what they model with some scenarios to see if the modeled structure can support various operational flows. For example, one Resident, for whatever medical reasons, goes to and from the Facility as follows:

1. Resident arrives without any External Clinical Records.

2. Resident leaves the Facility.

3. Resident returns after one month without any External Clinical Records.

4. Resident leaves the Facility.

5. Resident returns after seven days with External Clinical Records.

6. Test results (that is, External Clinical Records) for this Resident return to the facility five days later.

7. Resident leaves the Facility.

8. Resident returns two months later with External Clinical Records.

9. Resident leaves the Facility.

10. Resident returns six months later with no External Clinical Records.

What did the team learn from this scenario? The Clinical Records situation for this scenario is shown graphically, stepping through the above flow, in Table 5–1. This table shows when clinical records are created, the state (open, closed) of the various clinical records, how they move from open to closed over time, and how they would be linked in the above scenario.

Table 5–1   State of Clinical Records per Sample Scenario*

Step	Open Clinical Records	Closed Clinical Records
1. Resident arrives without any External Clinical Records.	I1	
2. Resident leaves Facility.	I1	
3. Resident returns after one month without any External Clinical Records.	I2 —— Linked to ——→	I1
4. Resident leaves Facility.	I2 ———————→	I1
5. Resident returns after seven days with External Clinical Records.	E1 I2 ———————→	I1
6. Test results (External Clinical Records) return to Facility five days later.	E2 E1 I2 ———————→	I1
7. Resident leaves Facility.	E2 E1 I2 ———————→	I1
8. Resident returns two months later with External Clinical Records.	E3 ———→ E2 ⟍ E1 ⟋ I2 ⟍ I1	
9. Resident leaves Facility.	E3 ———→ E2 ⟍ E1 ⟋ I2 ⟍ I1	
10. Resident returns six months later with no External Clinical Records.	I3 ———→ E3 ⟍ E2 ⟋ E1 ⟍ I1 / I2	

*Internal Clinical Records are labeled I1, I2, and so on, and External Clinical Records are labeled E1, E2, and so on.

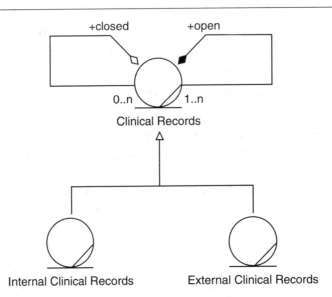

Figure 5–4 Final business object model for Manage Clinical Records (Part 2)

Two interesting items learned from this exercise are that:

1. The open clinical records can actually contain more than one set of External Clinical Records (step 6).

2. Newly created Internal Clinical Records may also need to be linked to closed Clinical Records (not just new External Clinical Records) (step 10).

Putting all this together, the team created a new model for the relationships among Clinical Records (Figure 5-4). This shows, as we were told by the business people, that there are two types of Clinical Records—Internal and External. Closed Clinical Records may be linked to other Clinical Records (Internal or External). Open Clinical Records contain other Clinical Records (Internal or External). The team then used these changes to update the other relevant models (Figures 5-5, 5-6, and 5-7).

Now Back to Our Program

The development team now moves forward to first address the part of OMaR that deals with compliance with government regulations. This direction was chosen for two primary reasons: (1) EAB Healthcare must remain in compliance or the business risks being shut down, and (2) one of the most critical

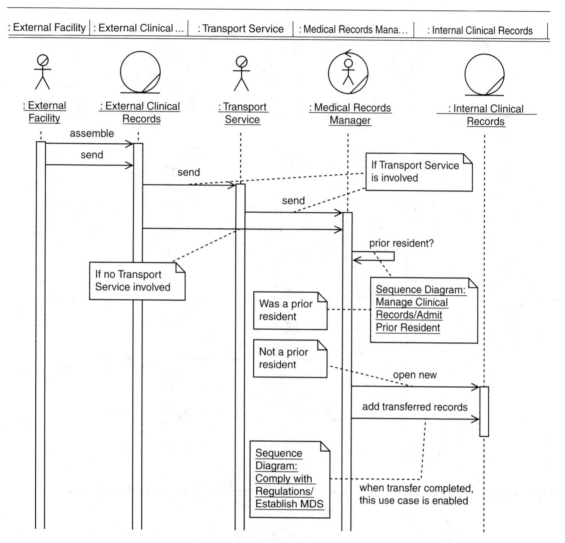

Figure 5–5 Updated sequence diagram for Transfer Records In (modified from Figure 3–13)

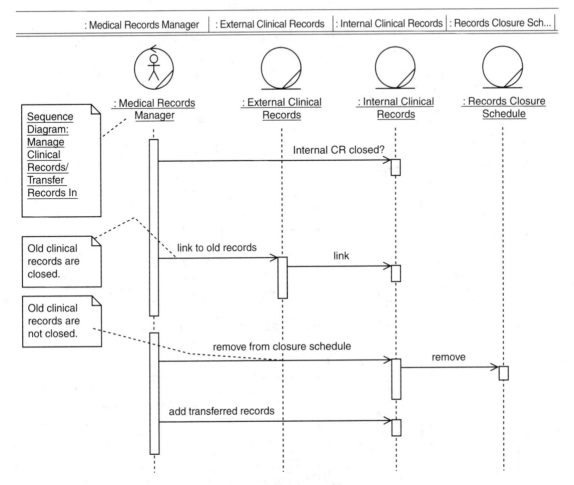

Figure 5–6 Updated sequence diagram for Admit Prior Resident (modified from Figure 3–15)

sections of the Clinical Records, the MDS, is central to EAB's operation. Each MDS contains data that provide a complete look at the condition of each resident. It is the one entity that is used most by the nursing staff, is used to create other important data entities, and is required to be updated and accurate to remain in compliance with regulations. The MDS is central to both the clinical and managerial operations of EAB Healthcare. Failure here would be disastrous. Therefore, the development team addresses this high-risk area first.

You will recall that within the Comply with Regulations subsystem three of its use cases were selected as high priority: Establish MDS, Maintain MDS, and Transmit MDS (Figure 5-8).

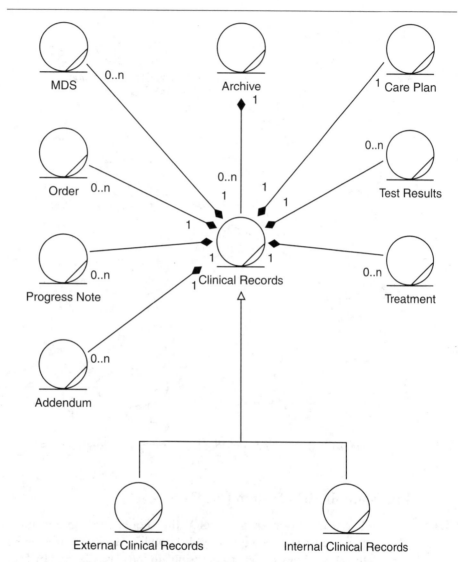

Figure 5–7   Updated traditional conceptual data model of Clinical Records (modified from Figure 3–21)

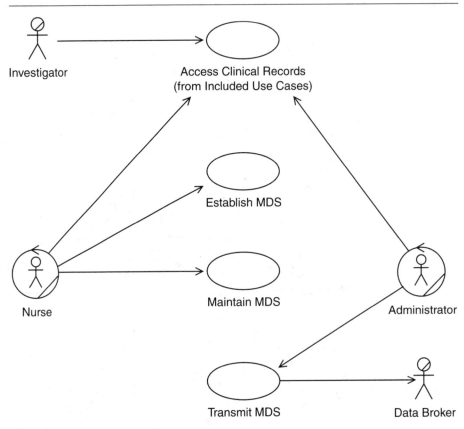

Figure 5–8   Use case model for Comply with Regulations

The Establish MDS System Use Case

The team proceeds to develop the sequence diagrams and class models for these use cases, beginning with Establish MDS. This use case is used to create the MDSs. They decide to prepopulate the class diagram by building the Nurse's view of this use case (the Nurse is the only actor using Establish MDS). They populate this view with entities with which the Nurse interacts when establishing the MDS (Figure 5-9). Such information can be found in the use case specification for Establish MDS.

Note that these entities are shown in the form of the typical class stereotype. Using this information the development team can now build the sequence diagram for the Establish MDS use case. The team members start by looking at the sequence diagram for the business use case Establish MDS. (By using sequence diagrams instead of activity diagrams in the business object

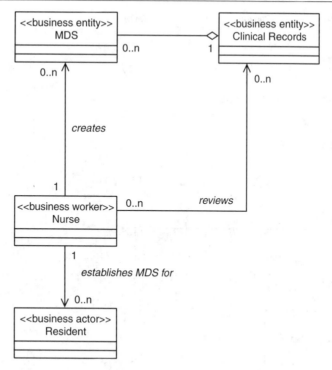

Figure 5–9 Nurse's view of Establish MDS

model, we can use the business-level sequence diagram to prepopulate the sequence diagram for the system use case Establish MDS.) Starting here they elaborate the Establish MDS system use case guided by the information in the use case description developed during requirements definition.

In addition to adjusting the basic message flow in the sequence diagrams, the team also adds additional processing regarding the linkage of current MDSs with prior MDSs. The knowledge that all MDSs for the same resident must be linked together was revealed during business modeling as part of the work on the Managing Clinical Records use case. Thus the team leaves the MDS linking function in the Manage Clinical Records / Admit Prior Resident sequence diagram (see Figure 5-6). That functionality is not required when creating new MDSs for new Residents (see Figure 5-10).

Also during business modeling the need for MDSs to be created and updated on certain timelines was established (see annotations on Figure 5-10). At that time the team members did not specify how this was to be accomplished (rightly so since in the business modeling and requirements definition phases they were establishing *what* was to be done, not *how*). This processing is not

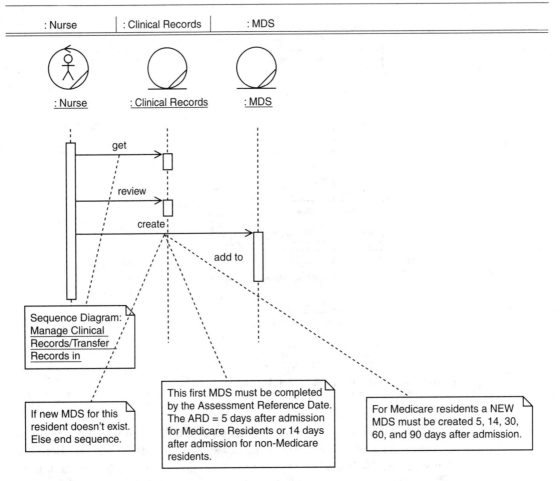

Figure 5–10 Sequence diagram for the Establish MDS system use case

included on this sequence diagram since it is not truly part of establishing an MDS, but establishing an MDS does trigger this processing. The team makes a preliminary design decision that this processing will run at night and report on MDSs that have not been updated according to the required timeline. (Note that they have not specified, at this time, the specific technology—background process, stored procedure, and so on—that will be used to do this.) The team documents this by updating the use case specification and by adding this into the class diagram (Figure 5–11) via a new control class, MDS Monitor. The team also creates a statechart diagram for the MDS Monitor class (Figure 5–12). This diagram specifies the locking and processing of the MDSs, including all the conditions upon which the MDSs will be logged as being in violation.

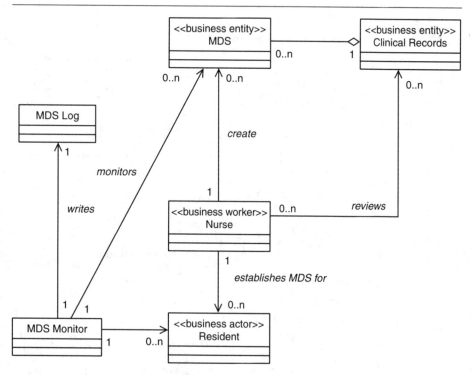

Figure 5–11 Updated class diagram (Nurse's view) for Establish MDS

The new MDS log simply is a report generated listing the MDSs that are out of compliance regarding the timelines for creating and updating them. The MDS Monitor class is a control class that is responsible for monitoring the timelines and reporting the violations.

From this point the team members begin to elaborate further details of the class diagram using all the information at hand and their development experience. For the purposes of Establish MDS, the Resident class merely holds basic identifying information about the Resident (obtained from supplementary specifications and discussions with the nursing staff). Little is done with the Clinical Records other than searching them for a specific resident or to add a new MDS (all from the sequence diagram). For the MDS class, typical basic operations are added beyond what was specified. Yet this is not a full definition of the MDS, only that which is needed for Establish MDS. The timeline parameters (that is, the business rules) for the creation and updating of the MDSs are added in the MDS Monitor class. Basic log information is added to the MDS Log. The Nurse class has little elaboration here since its only real interaction, other than requesting and providing clinical information, likely lies with the Access Clinical

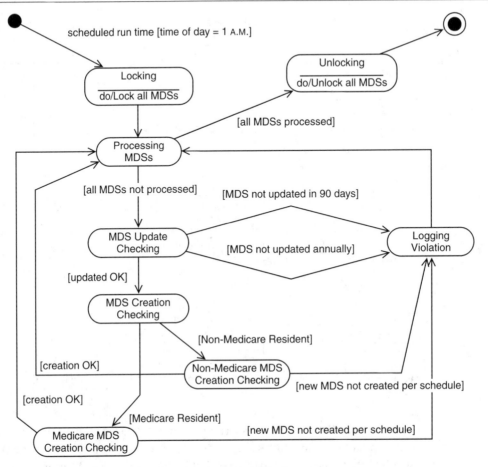

Figure 5–12 Statechart diagram for MDS Monitor

■ **Database Designer**

If you hadn't noticed, the MDS Monitor class is capturing key business rules for the system. As noted in the text, how the enforcement of these rules is to be accomplished has not been established yet. But having these rules modeled visually (instead of buried in a specification or hidden behind a model) allows you to immediately see that this is an area you may want to address. It depends on which side of the business rules argument you fall. If you want to enforce these rules in the database, the inclusion of this class in the model has put you on notice that it needs to be addressed. You should begin to do your analysis to determine where it would be best implemented—in the database, in the application, or within a separate business layer.

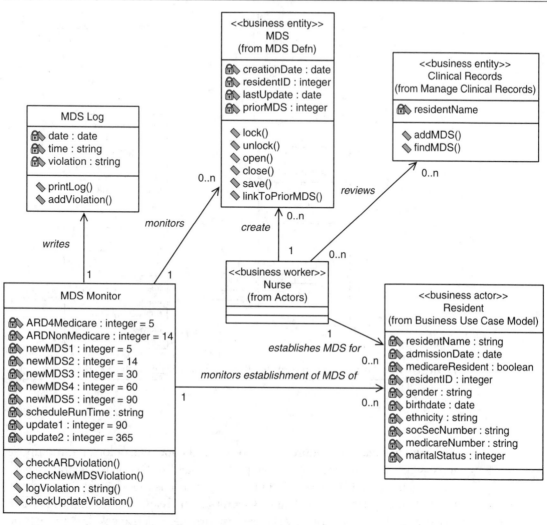

Figure 5–13 Class diagram for Establish MDS

Records use case. This will be elaborated upon when that use case is addressed. The resulting preliminary design class diagram is shown in Figure 5-13.

The Maintain MDS System Use Case

The team now proceeds in a similar fashion with the Maintain MDS system use case. The previously developed business use case description for Maintain MDS was left at a suspiciously high level of detail (see Appendix B). The team updates

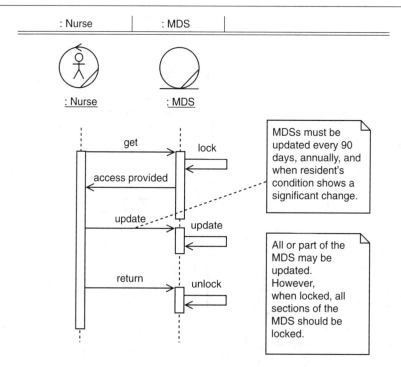

Figure 5–14 Sequence diagram for the Maintain MDS system use case

the sequence diagram (Figure 5-14) to add in the locking, unlocking, and updating insights that arose as they developed the Establish MDS class diagram.

This use case is very simple in that its purpose is to merely allow access to the MDS for updates by the Nurse. Given that, the team decides that the design as expressed in the Establish MDS use case provides such access and there is no need for an additional class model for Maintain MDS.

However, this sounds too simple to the team leader. She questions what it means to "maintain the MDS." The team members know from discussions with the business people and a quick look at some supplementary specifications on the MDS that it contains much information. Does the Nurse update the entire MDS or is it a partial update? If it is partial, can multiple Nurses update different sections of the MDS? Can they do this at the same time? Can any MDS be updated or only the newest one? The team leader decides that it's time to look closer at the MDS and assigns one of the analysts to build a UML model of the MDS, using the supplemental specs, so they can all see what they have.

She was correct. It was too simple. Even after reading the supplemental information, it was not apparent until they went back to the nursing staff that there is not just one type of MDS; there are many. Each is used for a different purpose and they coexist. Whether a Resident's records contain one or many types of MDSs, all the Resident's MDSs are referred to collectively as *the Minimum Data Set*. This lead to the initial class model of the MDS shown in Figure 5-15.

There is the Basic Assessment MDS that primarily provides identifying information. Thus you can see that the Resident class is part of the Basic Assessment MDS, as expressed by the aggregation. There is a Background MDS, which is typically created only once and contains some basic background information on the Resident. The Full Assessment MDS contains the bulk of the information, so much so that the team members decide to divide the Full Assessment MDS into three additional models. Thinking ahead to performance concerns, they use the criterion of the relative rate at which the individual sections of the MDS are updated: high, medium, or low (Figures 5-16, 5-17, and 5-18, respectively). The individual classes that represent the different sections of the MDS are then populated with attributes taken directly from the supplemental specifications. Each of these sections is relatively cohesive, representing one aspect of the Resident's condition (for example, Mood class, Medication class). For this primary reason the analyst chooses to represent each section as an individual class (versus one huge MDS class with everything in it). Note that this is not necessarily the way the MDS will be structured in the final data model. This is a representation of how it is composed in the current supplemental specifications provided by the business people.

Other information is gleaned from the business people during this uncovering of the MDS that answers the team leader's questions. Any given MDS update may be partial. The only items in the MDS that cannot be updated by the Nurse are the signatures and dates of the other staff personnel who have signed and dated the MDS. Only one Nurse can update an MDS at a time. Only the newest MDS can be updated (prior ones that have already been transmitted to the government are locked against update).

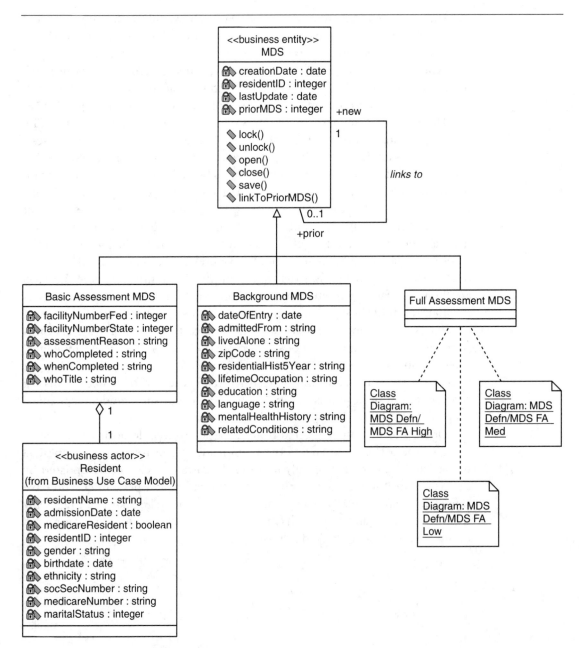

Figure 5–15   Initial class model for the MDS

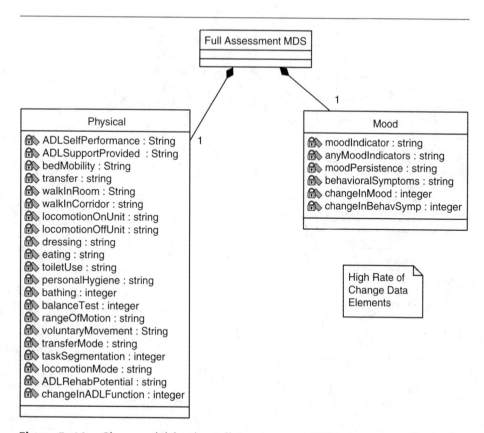

Figure 5–16   Class model for the Full Assessment MDS—elements with a high rate of change

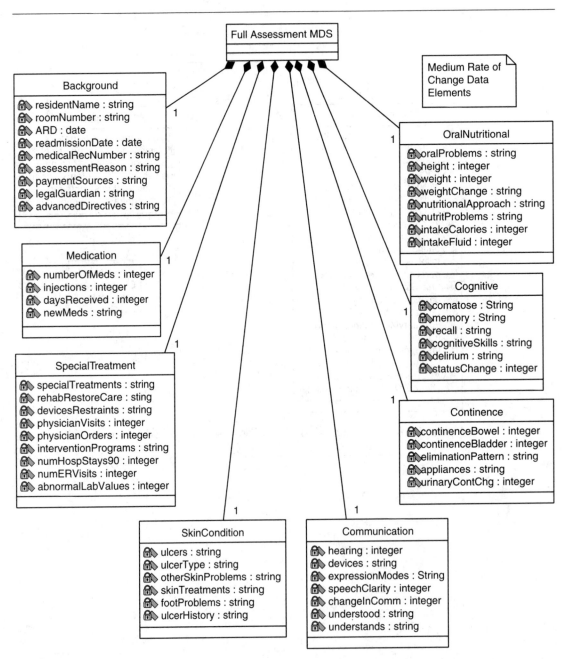

Figure 5–17 Class model for the Full Assessment MDS—elements with a medium rate of change

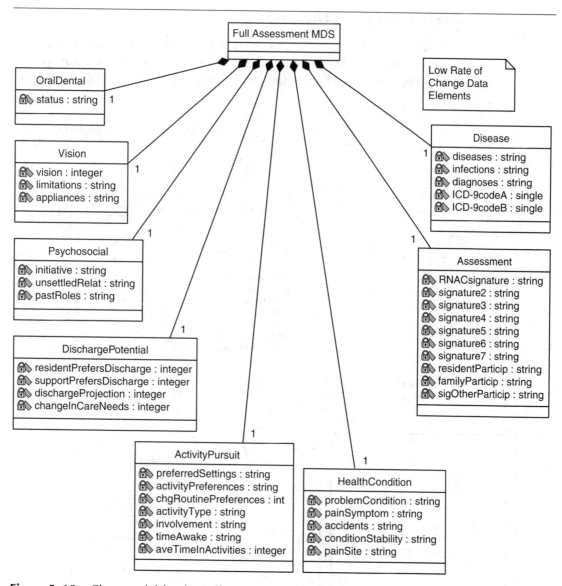

Figure 5–18 Class model for the Full Assessment MDS—elements with a low rate of change

The Transmit MDS System Use Case

The Transmit MDS system use case is for sending the updated MDS to the overseeing government agency for its review and approval. The team again updates the existing sequence diagram for this use case (Figure 5–19). Aside from some

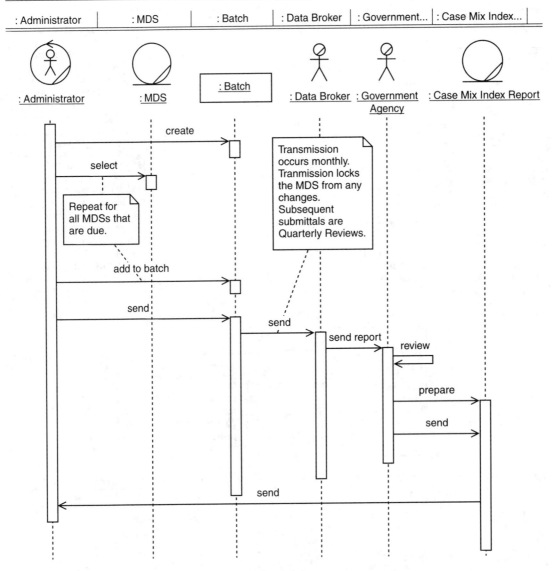

Figure 5–19 Sequence diagram for the Transmit MDS system use case

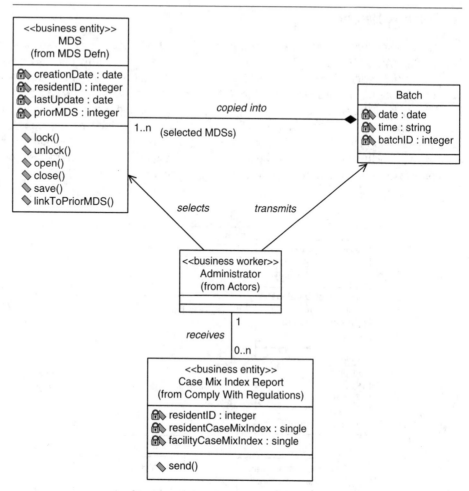

Figure 5–20 Class diagram for the Transmit MDS system use case

minor message flow changes, the team adds the concept of a "batch" of MDSs that are sent together as a group for approval.

Since all the dynamic behavior in this use case consists of operational activities (that is, activities performed by the facilities staff), the Administrator's view, created by the development team, becomes the class diagram for Transmit MDS (Figure 5-20).

As stated in the use case specification for the Transmit MDS system use case, and as seen in this class diagram, it is the Administrator who selects the MDSs to include in the batch to be transmitted.

■ Database Designer

At this point, the database designer raises a red flag. While the Batch class may be a good object-oriented representation of the set of MDSs being transmitted, there may be a better way. Recalling how critical this whole process is to the survival of EAB Healthcare and recalling the EAB staff mentioning how the transmission of the MDS sometimes fails (for reasons beyond EAB's control), the database designer suggests that Batch not be a fully transient class. He suggests that Batch be split into two classes: one persistent class, which will contain all the MDSs in the batch, and one transient class that handles the dynamic behavior of creating and transmitting the batch. Thus the Transmit MDS class model is modified as shown in Figure 5–21.

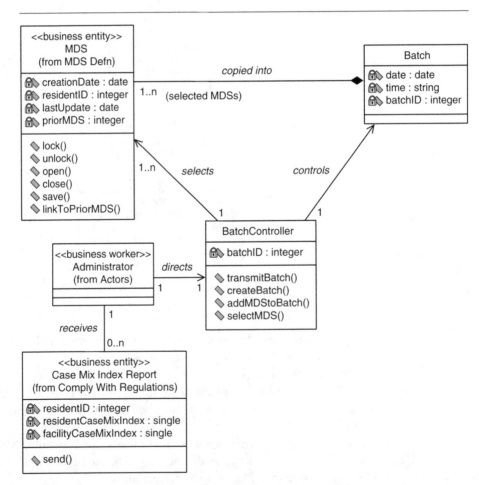

Figure 5–21 Updated class diagram for the Transmit MDS system use case

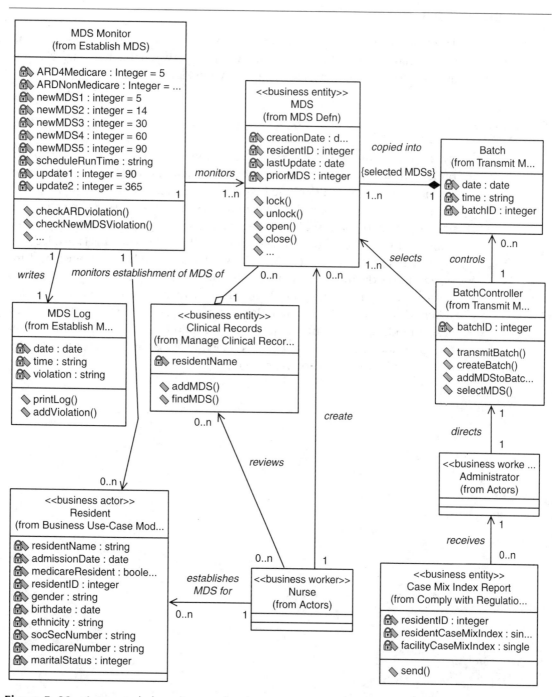

Figure 5–22 Integrated class diagram for the Transmit MDS system use case

Bringing It Together

The team decides to create an integrated view of the class models to ensure that nothing unusual was created, design-wise, between the individual class diagrams. The integrated class model is shown in Figure 5–22.

Summary

By leveraging the work that was already done in the previous phases of the project (business modeling and requirements definition), the work in the analysis and preliminary design phase is greatly simplified. Instead of beginning with a blank sheet of paper, key elements of the system already exist in the model (as use case, activity, class, sequence, and statechart diagrams and other specifications), waiting to be used. And when rework of previous designs is needed, having a common language (the UML) allows all team members to understand and respond quickly. In this way, the application and database teams, working together, get results faster and of higher quality than would have been typically achieved by working in separate development silos. The end result is a logical design model ready for the subject matter experts, the database designers, and the application developers to take over and move forward with the models that continue with their parts of the project.

Chapter 6

Preparing for Transformation to the Database Design Model

In this chapter, we begin to move from the logical analysis model to the database design model. This is the point where database designers start getting excited about thinking directly about the database itself. We look at the logical model and how it will transform to the first-cut data model, including the issues involved in mapping an object model to a data model.

The Workflow

Now we get to the point where the database designers begin to work within their subject matter expertise and the application developers begin working within theirs. Remember that this is an iterative process; the diagrams will not stay stagnant but should be expected to evolve as time passes, as new requirements are uncovered, and as the schedules change, causing feature changes.

There are two basic philosophies on where to go next. One camp says to change the logical design to become the object/class diagram that will represent the application directly, then map that part of the model directly to the data model. We have chosen to follow the second philosophy, which we present in this chapter. The appropriate teams continue to maintain the logical analysis model and the other models already created, but during this time the teams also move in two new directions: The development team builds its application design model based on the logical analysis model, and the database design team builds its model based on the same logical analysis model. This ensures that everybody is using the same base artifacts and that the metadata captured throughout the process continues forward.

Mapping Models

To understand how models change and mature over time based on the needs of the resulting application or database, it is important to maintain a mapping between the different diagrams. There are multiple ways to map models. In our scenario, we will map both the application and database design models to the logical analysis model, and we'll also map the application design model directly to the data model. This will give us the ability to understand some important information: how the models change based on how the subject matter experts see changes needed for their areas, how the iterations made to the requirements affect the logical design model, and how to map the object model to the data models to help build data access in later iterations.

Specifically, it is not really the model you are mapping but the elements within the models. You will be mapping classes to tables, attributes to columns, types to datatypes, and associations to relationships, which will help the teams understand how the application will interact with the database. Not all elements in each model will be mapped. Only classes that are persistent will map to the database, and there may be derived attributes within those persistent classes that don't map to columns. For example, often there are attributes, such as Total_Sales, that are sums of multiple columns in the database but are never stored anywhere in the database. Rather than storing the attribute, it is just a calculation in the application.

Mapping Classes to Tables

There are four basic ways to map classes to tables: one-to-one, one-to-many, many-to-one, and many-to-many. You may map them differently for various reasons, including performance, security, ease of querying, database administrator preference, corporate standards, database-specific needs, or other reasons that you may have experienced.

There are also some mappings that occur based on general relational database methodologies: many-to-many associations, subtypes, supertypes, and association classes. Many-to-many associations must be broken into one-to-many relationships by creating an association table. It is good practice to have additional columns in an association table over and above the foreign keys based on the relationships with the parent tables. If you don't have a need for additional columns, generally you do not need the many-to-many and can just create a one-to-many relationship or an additional table that is not really an association table.

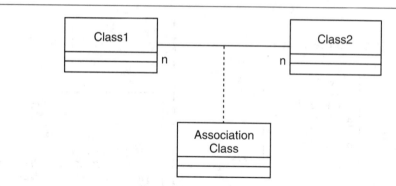

Figure 6–1   Association class in logical design model

If an association table exists in the data model and does contain columns in addition to the foreign key, there should be a related association class in the logical analysis model. One advantage to using the UML over traditional entity-relationship (ER) notations for the logical model is the support for an association class while still showing the many-to-many association (see Figure 6–1). Traditionally, in ER notations, you would either have just the association table, without the many-to-many, or not show the association table at all until you get to the physical database design model.

When mapping subtype classes to tables, you have three basic choices:

1. One table per class
2. One table per concrete class
3. One table per hierarchy

One table per class is quite simple. Each class is mapped directly to a corresponding table. One table per concrete class is also known as "rolling down" the supertype table into its subtypes. You take the attributes from the superclass and make them columns in tables that map to the subtype classes. One table per hierarchy is also known as "rolling up" the subtypes to the supertype. When rolling up the subtypes, you take the attributes in the subtype classes and map them to columns in a single table that maps to both the supertype and subtypes. Most of the time when rolling up tables, a new column or multiple new columns are created in the table to describe the original subtype tables. For example, there may be a set of classes with Employee as the parent and subclasses of PartTime and FullTime (see Figure 6–2). In the data model you may

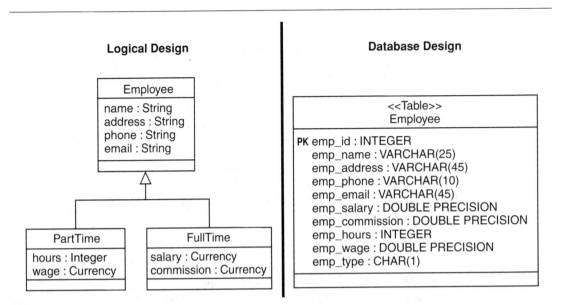

Figure 6–2   Transforming a class diagram inheritance hierarchy to one table per hierarchy in the database design

roll the tables all into the one Employee table, but there will be a new column created that doesn't really map to any attributes in the classes—emp_type. There may be a check constraint on emp_type of two valid values, part-time and full-time. This will allow the application to define the type of Employee without having to waste time querying three tables to find the Employee information. The application can just query one table and include the emp_type column.

Mapping Attributes to Columns

There are many ways to map attributes to columns. They don't affect just the column mapping; they also may affect the class-to-table mapping. You may have attributes that don't exist in the database or columns that are never really shown or even cared about in the application, but they are there for database-specific needs. At times you will have an attribute, or possibly even a class, that maps to multiple columns in a database. For example, an Address class may map into Address1, Address2, City, State, Country, PostalCode, and so on.

When mapping the attributes to columns, database performance may be taken into account, but more often the needs of the data drive the process. You may even involve database views in this scenario so that you can map attributes as part of a class to a table or just some columns. This is done mainly for easy access to the columns that are frequently queried or for security reasons. In most databases, you cannot assign security to an individual column but only to the entire table. Therefore, views become very important to secure the data. Employee information such as salary is not something that is going to be given to everyone who needs to access employee information. Thus there may be a view for specific users which has only the specific employee information needed. That way these users cannot access the salary information.

Mapping attributes to columns does come in partly under the class-to-table mapping, and both must be considered in either case. You cannot change columns without affecting tables, and you cannot change tables without affecting columns. You may have a class that has methods for looking up address information based on the input of a postal code. The database doesn't care about the lookup algorithm, just that it needs all the address information. The application, on the other hand, may have this setup in two classes, one for the address and one for postal code lookup (Figure 6–3).

An application may contain a calculation for computing total sales, but this never exists in the database. The database is concerned with sales specific to a product or region, and the application calculates any other combinations needed for data retrieval. Attributes that base their value on calculations of data retrieved from the database are called *derived attributes* and do not persist within the database.

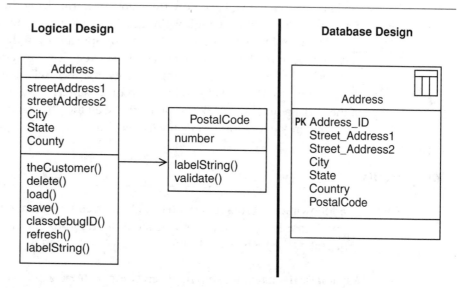

Figure 6–3 Class diagram with a lookup class for postal code and its representation in database tables and columns

When mapping attributes to columns, it is important not just to map the column name(s) but also to understand how analysis datatypes will map to the datatypes specific to your database choice. Analysis datatypes are meant to be generic, or logical, so that you do not need any expertise in specific software (for example, Oracle, IBM DB2, Microsoft SQL Server, and so on) but just the subject knowledge of types on your attributes. These may include such generic types as String, Date, Currency, and Integer, among others. When involved in analysis, it isn't as important to always understand the lengths for precision needed on a datatype as to begin the definition of the attribute.

When mapping these attributes to the specific database columns, you will then need to expand the columns to include these elements as well as possibly check constraints to further define the columns. For example, you may have a column, Country, for which you want to create a valid value check constraint that lists all countries that can be entered within that column. This is also when you may need to make an architectural call about where the business rules really get enforced. You can enforce them in the application as a method or group of methods, in the database as check constraints, or in a business layer so that you can change the rule without changing either the application or the database.

The Case Study Status

As EAB Healthcare begins to consider its options moving forward to database implementation, we will see how the plans for normalizing the existing logical analysis models continue and begin moving the logical models into database design models. In this chapter, we do not look specifically at the ways data modeling is done in the UML, but we plan for the next chapter, where the data model is specifically created by modeling the database as it will exist. The database design team at EAB needs to go back and make sure that a good understanding of the initial requirements exists among the team members and that iterations of those requirements and recently uncovered requirements are spelled out clearly.

The Concepts

The following UML, object-oriented, and other concepts are cited in this chapter. For a more complete discussion and more rigorous definitions of UML concepts, refer to Booch et al. [1999].

Association—a relationship between two or more elements that represents a link between instances of those elements

Aggregation—a special form of association that specifies a "whole–part" relationship between the whole and its parts

Association class—a modeling element that has both association and class properties

Generalization—a relationship in which objects of the child are substitutable for objects of the parent; represents an "is a" relationship between the super- and subtypes

Inheritance—the mechanism by which more specific elements incorporate the structure and behavior of more general elements

The Approach

At this point the teams begin working in their expert domains. The database designer will start to normalize the logical design and prepare it for the database design. Unlike the previous chapters, we now focus, for the most part, fully on the database designer's activities. (Thus there is no longer the need to use the special sections to highlight key areas for the database designer.)

The first step is to work through the logical class diagram to normalize it so that it can be used to create the database design model. Depending on the process, you may create separate entities that are mapped to the current class diagram, but for our example, we will work with the current class diagram and normalize it. While this process is ongoing, the design aspects can begin for both the application designs and database implementation designs. These designs will be built from the logical analysis model while maintaining a link back (see Figure 6–4).

There is a need to understand the classes within the model and to make sure that everything needed exists. As a logical data model, there may be a need to define some of the classes that were created as not needed in the database. We will assign a UML tagged value of persistent to all classes that we want to transform to the database. At the same time, there may be attributes that will exist only in the application. Therefore we want to keep them in the logical analysis model but not have them exist anywhere in the database. For example, a database may keep track of individual billing information or may even break it down to specifics within a resident's stay, but the accounting staff wants a quick way to see what Medicare is going to pay. So we create a derived attribute called TotalMedicarePaymentDue, an attribute that, along with a method, calculates the total amount due from Medicare and exists only in the application. There may be a very good business reason for creating this attribute and it may satisfy a requirement, but it is not captured in the database.

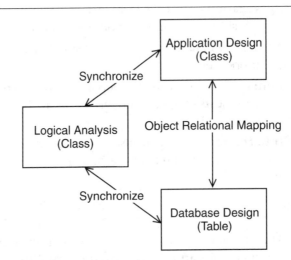

Figure 6–4 Linkage between the logical analysis, database design, and application design models

Inheritance or generalizations become a factor at this stage as well. When in the logical analysis model, we need to make sure that every instance can be modeled and understood. In the MDS, there are some attributes that are collected at different times for all residents. Therefore, we have a class as a supertype of MDS and two classes as subtypes: BasicAssessment and FullAssessment. This allows us to be sure, in an analysis phase, that we are capturing the information needed. When we begin to transform this to the database design models, we have decisions to make. Do we roll up the tables all into one, roll them down into the subtypes, or just leave them as is in a one-to-one relationship?

Discussions can become quite controversial depending on individual style or corporate methodologies. Other considerations are when to assign datatypes and unique identifiers or primary keys. Some camps say that the unique identifier is important only during implementation of the database, so they wait for the database design model. Others want it earlier to make sure the database is fully normalized prior to denormalization. At EAB, the data analysis team in the logical analysis model will define the primary keys. Also, the datatypes will be non-database-specific types, defined at the logical level, which will be further defined and mapped during database implementation.

The last step during the analysis phase, so that we can transform properly to the database design model, is to ensure that each class defines only one thing. The concept of normalization includes the requirement that each class or entity must define only one subject and should not cross subjects. If the class defines more than one thing, it should be split into multiple classes. During the process of working on the database design diagram, tables may be combined for reasons of optimization. But to make sure that the model is normalized first and that we are capturing all data needed, we have to analyze the model to make sure that each class is unique in the type of data it is capturing.

The Design

It is time for the database design team at EAB Healthcare to make some strategic decisions. What classes from the logical analysis model will be transformed into the data model? How will they become tables? Without consideration for the specific relational database management system (RDBMS) to be chosen or performance issues, it is time to know exactly what data will be captured. In the previous chapters, the business analysts, application developers, and database designers worked together to understand the requirements for the system and what problems it would solve. Now the database designers take their piece and begin moving forward. The process follows a basic flow, but as always, development is an iterative process, and there most likely will be steps that begin now but are continued later, during or after other processes.

Making Entities Persistent

Members of the database design team have been working with the representatives from other parts of the development organization to define elements of requirements, business rules, classes, and more. Now the database design team will work with or at a minimum consult with the other teams to look specifically at those classes and decide what is to be marked as persistent and transformed to the data model. When using a UML design tool, the persistent tagged value can be set within the tool. It may even support transformation to a database design automatically or even the generation of Data Definition Language (DDL) based on the classes marked as persistent.

There are a lot of classes that have been defined throughout the process of gathering requirements and creating the logical design. Because the entire business of EAB is so large and there can be many different integrated systems working together, the database team thinks it best to look specifically at what is needed to support the MDS, working just on that issue for this first task. The MDS most likely will be contained within its own schema and possibly linked to other schemas as well. Although the focus for now is on MDS-specific information, there will be more global entities that will also be used outside of the MDS and are more global entities, for example, residentName. There will probably be a schema that covers generic resident information that will contain the resident's name, but we need to link to that to complete the MDS. So the database design team, although looking at the specifics needed for the MDS, either may capture this global type of information and link to existing systems or may have to build additional tables or schemas to support it. We will see the results of this in upcoming chapters, but for this chapter we focus on all that is needed to build a complete MDS.

The MDS is divided into three basic sections, the Basic Assessment Tracking Form, the Background Information, and the Full Assessment Form. Although there are three forms, the information for them will be captured together in one place. The forms are to be created in applications or the user interface, but it is all the same information and therefore will be captured in one database. It is important not to separate this information into multiple databases, so that if new forms must be developed that include information from multiple areas, it is much easier to reuse the structures already available and working. Looking at the classes already created, it is a fairly simple process to complete this first step to understand and define which classes will be turned into tables and columns.

By just working through the diagrams in the order they were created, the database designers make some decisions on which classes will be marked persistent:

Resident	Physician	Nurse
Insurance Company	Payor	Basic Assessment MDS
MDS	Guardian	Background MDS
Full Assessment MDS		

To drill down on the MDS, the database designers look at what is needed specifically for each MDS. The Background MDS and Basic Assessment MDS are fairly simple and mostly covered by the classes already marked, but the Full Assessment MDS is much more detailed and requires a lot of information. Therefore, many more classes must be marked as persistent. The Full Assessment MDS covers the resident's entire history, the family history, and current problems (both in physical and mental health); daily routines; and more. We will not list each of the classes separately, but they will be marked and used later in the database.

Transformation of Attributes

There are choices to be made on which attributes will eventually become columns in the database. There are attributes that will not become columns and columns that will be created once the database design model begins to take shape. Different methodologies have their own theories on primary and foreign key participation in the logical analysis model, but for our model, we will have a mix of primary keys in the logical analysis model. There will be some primary keys, where they are needed, but some will be created in the database design model where the identifier is not needed for any other reason than to identify the table. Foreign keys will not exist in the logical analysis model. They will be created based on the relationships that appear in the database design model.

The database design team at EAB has been working closely with—and some members have even been a part of—the business analyst team. Now the design teams are reaping those benefits. The logical analysis model is well attributed and has the major information needed to move forward into the database design. The attributes at this point are all needed in the database design, so there aren't any marked as derived, although there may be some created by the application design team later that will appear only in the application. There are some classes that contain attributes that will become primary keys, for example, the business actor that will become a Resident table. Resident has an attribute called residentID, which is a unique identifier for each Resident and therefore will work perfectly as our primary key in the database design (see Figure 6-5). To mark an attribute as a primary key, the attribute can be marked with a tagged value, Part of Object Identity. This means that the attribute residentID is a part of the object identity for this particular class and it should become the primary key in the database design.

Resident
residentName : String
admissionDate : Date
medicareResident : Boolean
residentID : Integer
gender : String
birthdate : Date
ethnicity : String
socSecNumber : String
medicareNumber : String
maritalStatus : Byte
educationLevel : Byte
lifetimeOccupation : String
language : String
priorZipCode : String

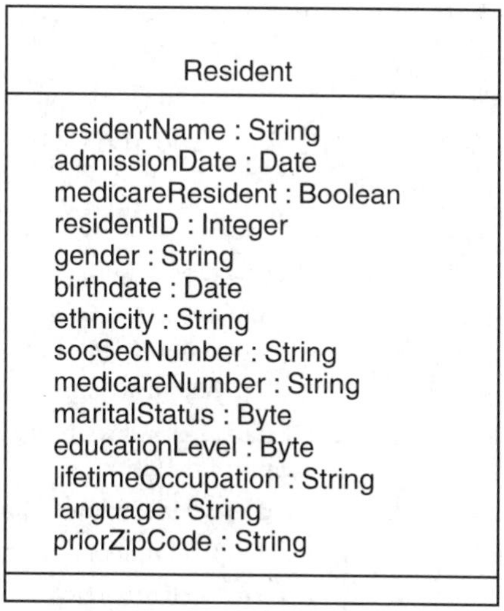

Figure 6–5   Resident class, fully attributed

We must also consider types. Logical analysis models generally contain attributes that have generic types or analysis types. These types are fairly descriptive but not specific to any implementation. There are some basic types; however, you can always add some of your own based on corporate standards or just personal or group preference. Many of the generic types made available in most tools are shown in Table 6–1.

Another way to use types is through the use of domains. Domains provide a mechanism to create user-defined types that are reused throughout the models. The domains contain all information that is associated with an attribute or column with the exception of the attribute or column name. Domains can also be very helpful in the transformation between the logical and database design models. Using domains to their fullest potential, you can define their properties for all types of models, including logical, database, or application, making the transformation between models almost seamless. In the next chapter we cover the modeling of domains and their usage in more detail. The EAB teams have not yet employed the use of domains within their design, but they have taken advantage of the many generic types.

EAB Healthcare has created a mapping of the logical types to the specific database types (Table 6–2). The database designers will ensure that when the transformation to the database design model occurs, the mapping will remain intact. The mapping of types is a very important function because if you do not use each generic type correctly, the data being captured may not match what was originally called for in the requirements. There is a need to map not only to the ANSI types but also, more importantly, to your specific database engine. It is quite helpful, though, to map to the ANSI types first because they generally map

Table 6–1 Generic Types and Their Descriptions

Generic Type	Description of Generic Type
Boolean	Used to represent the logical values of True or False
Currency	Used to declare variables capable of holding fixed-point numbers with 15 digits to the left of the decimal point and 4 digits to the right
Date	Used to hold date and time values
Double	Used to declare variables capable of holding real numbers with 15–16 digits of precision
Integer	Used to declare whole numbers with up to 4 digits of precision
Long	Used to hold numbers with up to 10 digits of precision
Single	Used to declare variables capable of holding real numbers with up to 7 digits of precision
String	Used to hold an unlimited number of characters

Table 6–2   Generic Types Mapped to ANSI SQL 92 Datatypes

Generic Type	*ANSI SQL 92 Datatype*
Boolean	Bit
Currency	Decimal
Date	Date
Double	Double Precision
Integer	Decimal
Long	Decimal
Single	Decimal
String	Char

well to any database engine available. The importance in the use of domains becomes more apparent here as well. It becomes obvious that if there is a need to manage the mappings, especially the length, precision, scale, and other properties of a column's datatype, it is nice to have something that is reusable and able to be defined exactly as planned, rather than a generic mapping.

Summary

Understanding the requirements early has given a great advantage in beginning the process of transformation from the logical analysis to the database-specific design models. Using the same logical design as the application developers makes work easier going forward as well. It is much easier to understand the object relational mappings, to ensure that the elements to be used in the database and application are defined once, and to guarantee that each element is the same, no matter who uses it. Understanding how the logical elements will map into the database will help the current project to proceed and speed up future projects as well. The job of the database designers was made easier by having a team with vast experience building the logical model. They built a design that was detailed and had the major functions already built in, for example, inheritance, generic types, normalization of classes, and more. The next step is to do the transformation from the logical model to the database design.

Chapter 7

Database Design Models— the UML Profile for Database Design

In this chapter, we look at the process of moving from the logical design models into the database-specific designs and what happens once we get there. Also included in this chapter is the new UML Profile for Database Design created by Rational Software Corporation for use when designing a database. We look at the stereotypes used in the UML for database-specific needs, how they are implemented, and how EAB Healthcare has used the UML and specifically the Profile to model the company's database needs.

The Workflow

The use of modeling to design databases far exceeds the use of modeling for applications and is generally done within most organizations with which we have worked and visited. The issue is that modeling a database is generally just that—modeling the database tables, columns, and relationships but not the entire database design. In this book, we look at many other parts of database design that can be modeled and how using the UML helps to model the entire database design. One part of database design that has not been covered very well in the past by the UML is the actual modeling of the database. Designers have primarily focused on using the UML for object-oriented application design and not for database design. With the use of the Profile for Database Design, this has helped open the UML to database design and database designers to the UML. Some tools like Rational Rose automate many of the stereotypes that we discuss so that the database designer does not need to understand the entire UML or even the stereotypes; designers can just take advantage of the UML without having to be experts.

We will model the database so that we can visualize and understand how the tables are structured and how they relate to other tables and views. Using the UML for the database design, we will also model constraints, triggers, schemas, indexes, stored procedures, and more. In the next chapter we will cover how to model the storage of the data, including tablespaces, databases, and partitioning.

Having a model of the database is important for many users. The database designer uses the data model in order to ensure database rules, including normalization, key migration, and others. The application developer can use the data model, especially if designed in the UML and mapped to the application model, to understand how the application accesses the database. This will help when the application developer is charged with building the data access software. A user interface (UI) developer also takes advantage of the data model to be sure that the UI picks up the available columns and uses the proper lengths, precision, and scale when designing the look and feel of the application. The analysts and end users (customers) use the data model to ensure that the data they believe is needed is captured in the database, in the correct format, to ensure fewer iterations.

During database design we begin to look at the specifics of the database so that we can decide what is being built and how to optimize it fully. This includes the type of server, operating system, database management software (DBMS) and version, and possibly other considerations. The selection of the DBMS will affect how optimization of the database is accomplished once the physical model is designed. Different DBMS systems consider different options for optimization, and the database administrator (DBA) works differently with their schemas depending on the DBMS chosen. For example, DB2 and Oracle are very sophisticated when it comes to storage, while SQL Server has been made more simplistic and doesn't offer nearly as many options, requiring fewer decisions to be made. Because of the different storage mechanisms used, the indexing specifically is treated differently, but there are many other options to consider, such as view support, triggers, stored procedure languages, and more.

Working as a Team

We have already discussed many ways that using the UML to do all of your modeling in one language is helpful in bringing the many teams involved in the development process together, but using the UML for modeling the database itself is helpful in its own right. The database is generally built by a team of data analysts, database designers, and database administrators along with others, and there must be a way for them to work together while building the database. The database teams themselves need to work together as a team, sharing artifacts, corporate and group standards, templates, diagrams, domains, and descriptions.

The standard entity-relationship (ER) notations do support the needs of the database team at this level, but the UML supports what ER notations support and beyond. The UML was built with ER in mind. ER modeling has existed for a long time, and when Booch, Rumbaugh, and Jacobson created the UML, they built it as a superset of ER notations. Since their intentions were somewhat different from those of database designers, supporting object-oriented development and not database design, some key needs of the database team were left out. With the addition of the UML Profile for Database Design, the UML supports the business models, the requirements models, and the logical and physical application and data models all in one language.

UML Packages

The constructs of the UML, beginning with the concept of packages, encourage sharing of information. By using packages a modeler can logically group information and break up the model artifacts in different ways for different uses. Often teams break up the model into standards packages and packages that different people or teams work on for different parts of the project, different phases (for example, development, testing, and production), and many other groupings that you can use to help make your job and communication among your team members easier (see Figures 7-1 and 7-2).

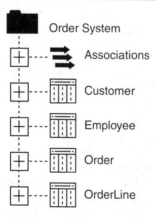

Figure 7–1 Tree browser showing a package structure

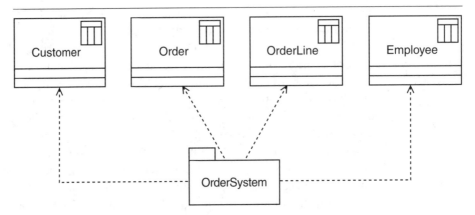

Figure 7–2 A diagram to visualize the elements residing inside the package

Packages can include different types of UML objects as well. A package can contain tables and classes, so that you can see visually and organizationally which tables map to which classes. Some modelers have logical design and database design packages so that they can easily see what is used during each phase of the project. Packages can be used as a good way to organize the models for version control, based on the package rather than on individual tables, for example. This way when you start using the model, you know exactly which elements are needed based on the package with which you begin. Having standard elements, such as domains, tables, classes, use cases, and others, stored in standards packages gives a way to understand the standards that can be used in new and existing models. Also, if you are using some sort of configuration management, you can version packages and be sure that they are maintained and not changed on a whim. Packages should be used to store standard modeling elements. The UML supports a derived relationship, which can be created from those standards to the elements that use them, helping to ensure that the elements are updated by changing the standard package. Some tools even support the changes automatically based on the association between the standard elements and the elements to which they are related.

UML Diagrams

The database design model represents the physical database design as it will be implemented in the DBMS. The database design is modeled in a new diagram type, called the *database diagram,* provided by the UML Profile for Database Design. Another advantage to the UML is that diagrams do not have to be typed; this means you can have elements of many different types on a diagram, or you can stereotype the diagram to a specific type and allow only those types of elements. You will often want a diagram that shows tables and to what tablespaces they belong. Having them both on the same diagram allows for the ability to understand which tables are in which tablespaces and whether they are partitioned across multiple tablespaces as well.

A typed diagram also can be helpful. Having a diagram with only specific items allowed makes it easier for the modelers to see which elements can be used on the diagram. Some tools supply typed diagrams that give you only the elements that apply to that diagram according to the UML. For example, a diagram typed as <<Database Diagram>> would include tables, relationships, views, stored procedures, and domains on that particular diagram but would not allow for things like classes, objects, and other nondatabase elements.

Database Design

Designing the database through data modeling in the UML gives you the ability to capture many more items on the diagram visually than with traditional ER notations. You can model elements like domains, stored procedures, triggers, and constraints as well as the traditional tables, columns, and relationships. There are several reasons to model the database, including creation of a good design, enforcement of referential integrity, management of standards reuse, and communication of the database structures. With the models used for these many areas and more, it is a tremendous advantage to describe visually on the diagram as many things as possible.

Database design is an iterative process; using models makes the constant change easier to manage and understand, allowing you to make changes to the models prior to code generation so you can understand what the implications are based on each change and analyze whether the change should be made or something else should be chosen. For example, a change to one relationship or key column could affect several tables based on that one single change. Because of key migration and the cascading of changes based on the key migration, one small change can cause data loss and incompatibility.

In a perfect world, there would always be what is called *model-driven development.* In model-driven development, all changes are made to the model prior to being implemented directly in the database. By using model-driven development, you can eliminate most surprises. You can see what the changes will affect prior to making the changes in the database directly. The problem is in reality; say the DBA gets a call in the middle of the night about a problem in the database or a call in the afternoon about something that isn't working or data that is missing. What does the DBA do? Go to the model, make the change, and then implement it? That's what we would like to see, but that isn't always possible. The DBA has to get the job done and doesn't have the time or desire to work in the model first, so he or she just changes the code and worries about the model later. This can cause problems that won't be uncovered until later when the database and model are resynchronized, but this is something that really can't be avoided.

The Case Study Status

Now that we have completed, at least for now, the logical design model for EAB Healthcare, we can move forward to the database design model and create a database design for the MDS in the UML. First it is important to understand the UML Profile for Database Design (see the "Concepts" section in this chapter). The Profile uses stereotypes and tagged values for all the information needed to describe the structures of the database and its elements. The Profile also uses constraints to enforce database design conformance. This includes many-to-many relationships not allowed on the database design, limiting them to the logical design.

EAB takes care of many residents, and since many of those residents receive government aid like Medicare and Medicaid, it is very important to keep a good record of all information on patients. If the residents' records are not well organized and easily queried, the government can fine EAB or even shut down the company. EAB's records are often scrutinized, so the creation of this new system will help satisfy many of the government's needs and protect EAB in the future.

The Concepts

The following UML, object-oriented, and other concepts are cited in this chapter. For a more complete discussion and more rigorous definitions of UML concepts, refer to Booch et al. [1999]. In this chapter we also cover many concepts that are not discussed in UML books and specifications that currently exist; these are part of the information in the UML Profile for Database Design. A profile is an extension to the UML that keeps the UML metamodel intact. The Profile for Database Design adds stereotypes and tagged values that are attached to the stereotypes but does not change the underlying metamodel for the UML. The Profile also includes some icons to more easily visualize the database elements that are created and rules to enforce about the creation of a relational database design.

The UML Profile for Database Design

In this chapter, we cover the first part of the Profile, how to model the database structures. In the next chapter, we will cover some of the more physical database elements involved in storage modeling. The database is created with tables, columns, and relationships. There are several elements that extend the database, like triggers, stored procedures, constraints, user-defined types (domains), views, and others. The Profile covers how to model all of these elements and where in the model they are defined.

Diagram Elements

The following diagram elements are described below. Figure 7-3 shows their associated icons.

Table—a grouping of information in a database about the same subject, made up of columns

Column—a component of a table that holds a single attribute of the table

Primary key—the candidate key that is chosen to identify rows in a table

Foreign key—a column or set of columns within a table that map to the primary key of another table

Identifying relationship—a relationship between two tables in which the child table must coexist with the parent table

Non-identifying relationship—a relationship between two tables in which each table can exist independently of the other

View—a virtual table that, from the user's perspective, behaves exactly like a typical table but has no independent existence of its own

Stored procedure—an independent procedural function that typically executes on the server

Domains—the valid set of values for an attribute or column

A table is a container composed of columns to store and organize the data in the system. A table is modeled as a class with the stereotype of table viewed as <<Table>>. The stereotype of table on class automatically causes all of the attributes on the class to become columns and automatically stereotypes the attribute as <<Column>>.

A column can be designated as a key or non-key column. A key column can be primary, foreign, or a combination of both primary and foreign. A primary key column is a column (or group of columns) that uniquely identifies its table or the row within its table. A foreign key is a column that was a primary key in a parent table that migrates to the child table and identifies the relationship between the tables. The foreign key can participate as a key or non-key column within the child table. The type of foreign key depends on the type of relationship involved

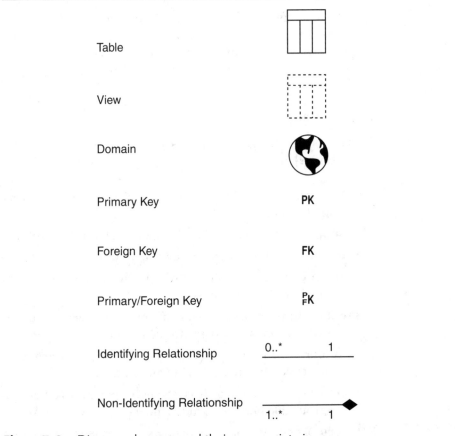

Table	
View	
Domain	
Primary Key	**PK**
Foreign Key	**FK**
Primary/Foreign Key	**^P_FK**
Identifying Relationship	0..* 1
Non-Identifying Relationship	1..* 1

Figure 7–3 Diagram elements and their appropriate icons

between the two tables. An identifying relationship between tables makes the foreign key part of the primary key in the child table; a non-identifying relationship makes the foreign key a non–primary key column. There are icons that help to visualize the tables, columns, and type of keys (see Figure 7-4).

There are two basic types of relationships when modeling the database: identifying (also known as mandatory) and non-identifying. The identifying relationship means that the child table cannot exist without the parent table. An example of an identifying relationship is that between Order and Customer; without a customer, the order doesn't exist. A non-identifying relationship occurs when the child table can live on its own. An example of a non-identifying relationship is that between Customer and Employee. A customer can exist without an employee, but often when an employee makes the sale that employee is assigned

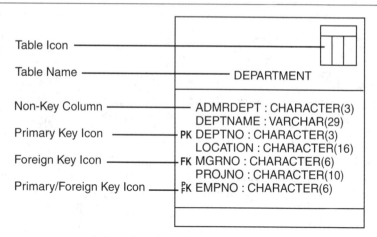

Table Icon

Table Name —————— DEPARTMENT

Non-Key Column —————— ADMRDEPT : CHARACTER(3)
DEPTNAME : VARCHAR(29)
Primary Key Icon —————— PK DEPTNO : CHARACTER(3)
LOCATION : CHARACTER(16)
Foreign Key Icon —————— FK MGRNO : CHARACTER(6)
PROJNO : CHARACTER(10)
Primary/Foreign Key Icon —————— PK EMPNO : CHARACTER(6)

Figure 7–4 Table with key and non-key columns

to the customer. With new technologies of the Internet and older technologies of catalogs, you may not have an employee who sold the product; the customer may have purchased it without employee assistance. Therefore it is not mandatory that a customer exist only when associated to an employee. The identifying relationship is created with a stereotype of <<Identifying>> on a composite aggregation, and a non-identifying relationship is created with a stereotype of <<Non-identifying>> on an association.

When creating relationships, there is a need to define the relationship with cardinality. Cardinality is a numerical range defined on the relationship on how many times the relationship can occur. An example using cardinality is one customer can place one or more orders. The UML shows the cardinality directly on the relationship. For this example it would look like a 1 on the customer end of the relationship and 1..* on the order end of the relationship. Because it is a 1 and not 0..1 on the parent end of the relationship, this means that the relationship cannot be null and that each customer must have at least one order. You can also define roles on a relationship. A role describes the relationship textually. For this same example, the roles would be read as a customer places one or more orders, with *places* being the role on the customer (see Figure 7-5).

Database views are defined as a database component that behaves exactly like a table but has no independent existence of its own. A view is also known as a virtual table. Views may have different rules depending on the database server. For example, in Oracle a view can be updated, whereas in SQL Server Version 7 it cannot. A view is defined in the UML as a class with the stereotype of <<view>>. The view can be derived from one or more tables or views. A

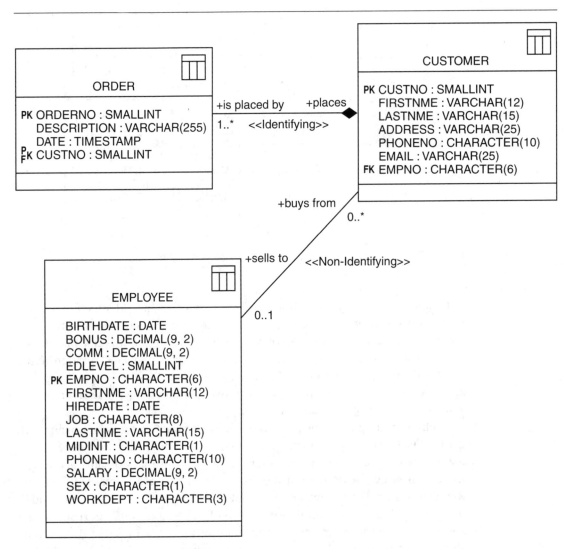

Figure 7–5 Employee, Customer, and Order tables and their relationships

view's relationship to its parent tables and views is modeled with a dependency with the stereotype of <<Derived>> (see Figure 7–6).

Another one of the many advantages of using the UML for your database design is the ability to model standard elements that are not generally modeled in traditional ER notations but have great value in being modeled. One such element in the database design is the stored procedures. A stored procedure can be defined in different ways, again based on the database server. The stored proce-

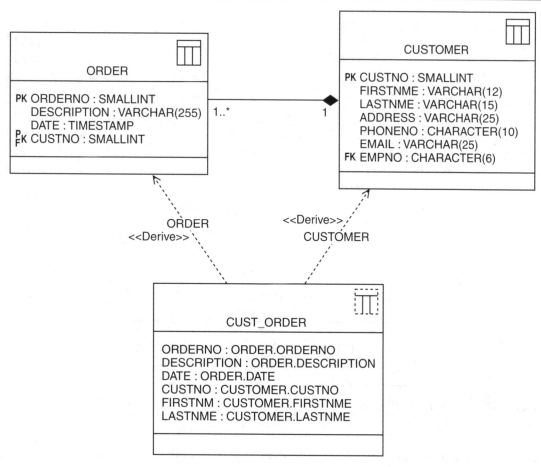

Figure 7–6   Model elements for a view and its relationships to parent tables

dure can be defined as a procedure within the database, from an external file or as a function. Some databases support the concept of a stored procedure package or container. A stored procedure container is a grouping of one or multiple stored procedures within a group and currently is supported in the Oracle 8i database. The container is modeled as a class with the stereotype of <<SP Container>>. Within a <<SP Container>> are stored procedures, which are modeled as operations on the container with the stereotype of <<SP>>. Another advantage of showing the procedures on the diagram is that you can visualize what the parameters are and the procedures dependency on tables within the database (see Figure 7-7).

When building a database design, it is important to enforce standards and enable ways to reuse elements as much as possible. The use of domains, also

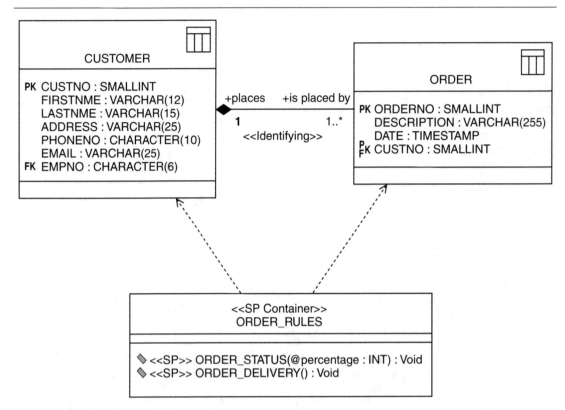

Figure 7–7 Stored procedure container Order_Rules, its stored procedures, and its dependencies

known as user-defined datatypes, gives the modelers the power to reuse elements. A domain has all of the properties of a column except the column's name. The domain is assigned to one or more columns and the column inherits all of the domain's properties. If you change the properties of the domain, it will change the properties of all columns that inherit from that domain. A domain can be used as a standard to be reused within one or several models. A domain is a class that has the stereotype of <<Domain>>. A domain has attributes, which pertain to a column's property. A composite domain can also be used, which is a class that has the stereotype of <<Domain>> but has multiple attributes. When a domain has multiple attributes and it is assigned to a column in a table, the additional attributes become columns as well. An example of a composite domain would be address. The domain address has attributes of street1, street2, city, state, country, and postal code. A table for customer has a column called address with the domain of address assigned to it. When the table is expanded for code generation, it will contain all of the columns of the address domain. This will enable a standard address to be used everywhere in the model.

Table and Column Elements

A table can contain many items in addition to the columns that have already been described. In the same way, columns contain many elements that have to be described as well as some that appear directly on the diagram. The elements of tables and columns that appear in the diagram are

Constraints—a rule that limits the value of or actions on the specified data field

Key—a constraint that defines a type of key and its column(s)

Check—a constraint that defines rules against the database

Unique—a constraint that defines a column or set of columns as containing unique data

Trigger—a code that tells the database what actions to perform

Index—a file that enables faster data access

Datatype—a type whose values have no identity

Precision—the maximum number of digits allowed for a numeric data item

Scale—the number of digits in the fractional part of a numeric data item

Length—the maximum number of letters allowed for a character data item

Null—a column that is not mandated to contain data

Not null—a column that must contain data

Other elements that are part of the tables and columns as tagged values but may not appear in the diagram themselves are

Owner—the creator of the database or specific element of the database

Comment—a description in a database

Identity—a column that has data automatically added by the database, generally for primary key columns

The UML supports the concept of tagged values. They can differ based on the stereotype of an element and the type of element. The stereotype inherits its own tagged values and can include some or all of the tagged values on the base element prior to the stereotype. As always, some of these tagged values vary depending on the database server, but within this book, we try to stay generic and stick to standard ANSI SQL rules.

There are three basic types of constraints and they can be assigned to a column, but generally they are owned by the table itself. The key constraint defines the primary and foreign keys for the table and can contain one or more columns. There are two different types of key constraints: primary key and foreign key. They are modeled as operations on a table with the stereotypes of <<PK>> and <<FK>> (see Figure 7–8). A check constraint is a rule on a column or table that can consist of calculations, a valid set of values, or a range of values. A check constraint is modeled as an operation on a table with a stereotype of <<Check>>. The last type of constraint is a unique constraint. A unique constraint designates that the data in a column or set of columns data must be unique. If a set of columns is grouped within a single unique constraint, the data when combined for the entire set of data must be unique, but the data within a single one of those columns are not required to be unique. A unique constraint is modeled as an operation on a table with the stereotype of <<Unique>>.

There are two types of triggers, one that is modeled and defined on a particular table and another that is part of a relationship to ensure proper referential integrity. This section covers the table-level triggers. They are created to trigger events to happen when something is done to a specific table. The trigger is database code that tells the database what other actions to perform after

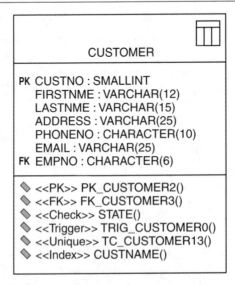

Figure 7–8 Customer table with constraint, trigger, and index operations and stereotypes

certain SQL statements have been executed. The table-level trigger is modeled as an operation on a table with the stereotype of <<Trigger>>. A trigger can have many tagged values that get stored in the model, but they vary significantly based on the database server and version being used. You can create the necessary tagged values as needed based on your particular database needs.

The final operation that is modeled on a table is the index. An index is a pointer used to locate rows in a table rapidly. You can think of an index as the folder tabs in a filing cabinet—an index allows you to file information in a certain place and makes it very quick to find the information you are seeking because it organizes what you need in a single place. An index is modeled as an operation on a table with the stereotype of <<Index>>. There may be some tagged values on an index, for example, an index can be unique and therefore it would contain the tagged value of unique.

Datatypes, precision, scale, length, and nullability are tagged values on columns but may be displayed on the diagram as well. It is quite useful to visualize these tagged values on the diagram so that you can easily understand what the values of a column are. It is just as important to be able to not display these values on the diagram so that when using the diagram for specific needs, it is less cluttered, easier to read, and less technical for some of the nontechnical viewers. There are no specific stereotypes for tagged values, but the list of values available depends on several items, including the stereotype and to what database server the table is attached.

Additional tagged values that may not be as useful on the diagram but are very important to the model itself are owner for the table, comment on all elements of the model, and identity, which is available to many databases as a rule on a column that automatically generates a sequence of unique values for a key column. Different databases call identity something different, but the concept is similar, so we have chosen one word to describe them all. An identity column generally can be an assigned tagged value of only certain datatypes and should be available for use only with those datatypes.

The Approach

The typical approach to moving into the actual modeling of the database is to use all of the classes that were already captured and understand how they will become tables. At this point the classes that will be transformed into tables should have been marked with a tagged value of persistent. This tagged value means that the class requires data and that the data for this class persists in the database. Therefore, the database must contain the needed structures to support the class. Having already worked through the requirements and an understanding of what is being built and how to describe it from both a business and a technical sense, it is much easier to determine what tables to create, the data and descriptions of those tables, and how to construct them.

Although the database design team has been involved with the previous requirements gathering and modeling of the needed elements, it is now time to look at the model from strictly the database point of view. The database designers look at the needs of the database from a more physical view. It is not yet quite the time to look at specific database server requirements, but we begin to understand what would make this a good optimized data model. For example, do all of the tables have unique identifiers? Is referential integrity being enforced through key migration? Are there rules within the database, from the earlier requirements, that may cause a need for constraints and stored procedures? Employ corporate and group standards to ensure that the database model meets the rules of the organization.

Since we are using the UML, an understanding of how models are built in the UML and perhaps a tool that supports database design using the UML are very helpful at this point. You can use the UML and any tools that support the creation of stereotypes to begin this process, but it is always easier if you already have the stereotypes and database knowledge so that the tool can get out of your way and the database designers can just start working on the model. Knowledge of the entire UML itself is quite helpful at this point as well, allowing the modelers not only to build their database models but also to use the existing models to understand what has been done and described so that the modelers can continue to use the requirements and definitions for those requirements that have already been described.

When building a database model, it is beneficial not to concern yourself with the physical aspects of the database until you are sure that all of the requirements have been captured and modeled as database elements. For this reason, we do not cover the physical storage of the data here, saving example schemas, tablespaces, databases, and other items until the next chapter. This chapter focuses on how to build the database model using the UML without a focus on implementation. However, the database designers begin to think about the implementation with the creation of views to store data for better access, constraints to enforce rules that were uncovered during the earlier processes as well as during database modeling, indexes based on query patterns that may have been uncovered in sequence diagrams, and stored procedures and triggers to enforce rules that have been identified.

The Design

The database design team first focuses on creating tables from existing classes. This ensures that all of the classes that were created and marked as persistent based on the requirements that were gathered are moved forward into the database. Once that has occurred, the team can start looking for ways to optimize the database, beginning with how to handle tables that were created based on inheritance relationships in the class model and classes that took part in many-to-many relationships that have to be split using association tables. From there the database design team will begin to ensure uniqueness of the tables and enforcement of such items as rules using constraints on the database. The database design team at EAB Healthcare doesn't really work much with triggers and stored procedures. They are handled primarily by the database administrators and will therefore be worked on later, after the database design model has been fairly locked down.

Creating Tables from Classes

EAB has done a good job of capturing the requirements and turning them into classes. Working together, the development, business, and database teams have gone through each of the classes and marked the ones that are needed as persistent. The first job for EAB's database designers in creating tables from classes is to decide what packages to work with and to begin the transformation to tables.

The database designers for EAB begin to move items into the database, working first with some of the actors that have information required for the MDS. Based on the government requirements, EAB has identified three primary MDSs that EAB has to be concerned with: the Background MDS, the Basic Assessment MDS, and the Full Assessment MDS. Each of these is important and feeds information to the other. When building the database, we want to begin with the lowest common denominator and build from there. This ensures that the basics are covered. As the database designers continue gathering the information that needs to be captured, they can determine whether each item needs its own table, can fit into an existing table, or is already being captured for another purpose.

The database team looks at the requirements for each MDS type to determine what information is needed to complete each type. It is almost like thinking of each MDS as some type of form or screen and considering what information is needed to fill in that screen and what is the best way to organize the information in table and column structures to store the information.

Background Information

The first set of information captured about a patient in the initial MDS comes from the background information obtained at admission. The Background MDS gathers the initial information from an incoming resident as he or she registers at EAB and can be used to fulfill much of the more detailed MDS later.

The background information is used to understand who the resident is and some of his or her habits, problems, and reasons for coming to EAB.

Based on the needs of the Background MDS, the information is broken into two categories:

1. Demographic information
2. Customary routine

The database design team creates a set of tables based on the typical information needed for these two categories, gathering the appropriate information from the classes and actors that already exist. The Resident actor fulfills most of the demographic information needed and the customary routine information is gathered from various other classes. Figure 7-9 shows the first database diagram the team creates to support the Background MDS.

For the transformation from the logical design model to the database design model, the team creates and uses some domains, as shown in Figure 7-9. The primary domain is Boolean and is mapped to a CHAR(2). Also attached to that domain is a check constraint that has a valid value of y or n. This helps to enforce that the logical type of Boolean is transformed correctly to a database type of CHAR(2) and has rules to enforce its properties.

Basic Assessment Tracking

The next set of information that is tracked and may have a set of circumstances for when it is used to feed the Full Assessment MDS is the Basic Assessment Tracking (BAT). Some of the information for the BAT will come from tables that have already been created in the Background MDS and some will be new. The database designers for EAB create diagrams to demonstrate each type of form. Tables can be included on many diagrams but exist only within one model. A diagram is a basic way to display information visually to make it easier to understand and group in a logical way.

The EAB database designers now focus on the BAT and transform classes to tables that pertain to the BAT. There is really only one class that becomes a table for the BAT, the Basic Assessment MDS class. The other table used in the diagram is the Resident table (see Figure 7-10).

Full Assessment Data

The final set of information needed to complete all of the information for the different types of MDSs is the Full Assessment MDS. Just like the previous sets of information, the Full Assessment MDS includes some information already

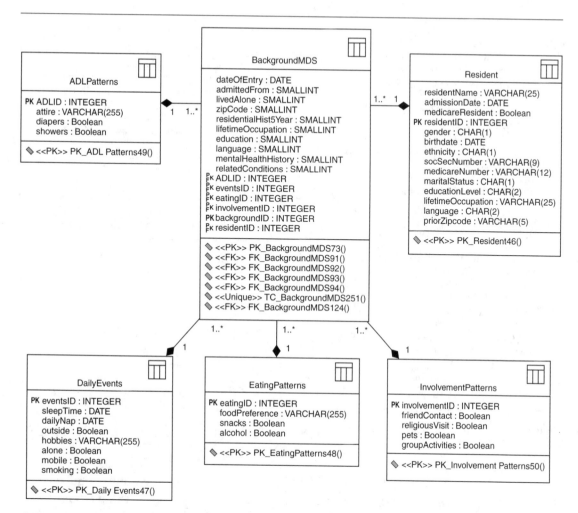

Figure 7–9 Database diagram for background information obtained at admission, shown prior to adding constraints

captured mixed with new data needed only for the Full Assessment MDS. The EAB database designers begin looking at the information already captured in the logical design that is needed to create the Full Assessment MDS and decide what to transform into the database design as tables and columns. Once the database designers have completed their assessment of the classes to become tables, they create the tables as needed and make sure that column properties are correct based on the business rules already uncovered and the needs of the database design.

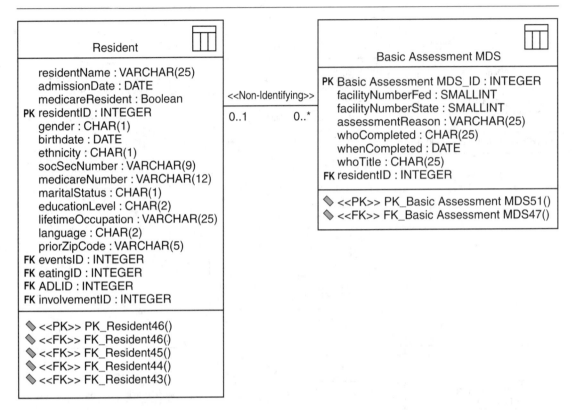

Figure 7–10 Database design diagram for the Basic Assessment Tracking

The Full Assessment MDS contains many tables, columns, and relationships—everything from the prior MDSs as well as everything from its own MDS—and therefore is quite crowded. The EAB database designers decide to build several diagrams to display the Full Assessment MDS to make it easier to read and understand. One diagram has a complete overview of the entire MDS but contains only table names and relationships (Figure 7-11). One diagram contains just the new tables that are involved in the Full Assessment MDS and not the tables involved in other MDSs (Figure 7-12). The database designers create several other diagrams for different views as well.

The database designers make several changes to the model to help make it more easily read and optimized. First they create alternate keys for the Background MDS, Full Assessment MDS, and Basic Assessment MDS, enabling the designers to migrate the alternate keys rather than all of the primary keys. This is a big change to the model because of all the identifying relationships from the child tables to each of the different types of MDS tables; there would have

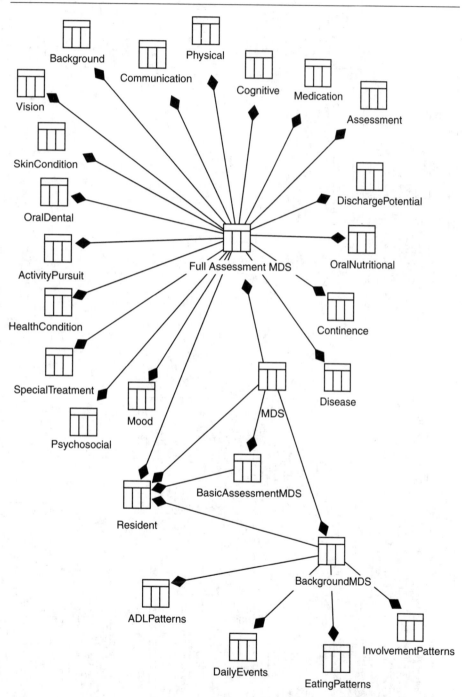

Figure 7–11 Complete overview diagram of the entire MDS

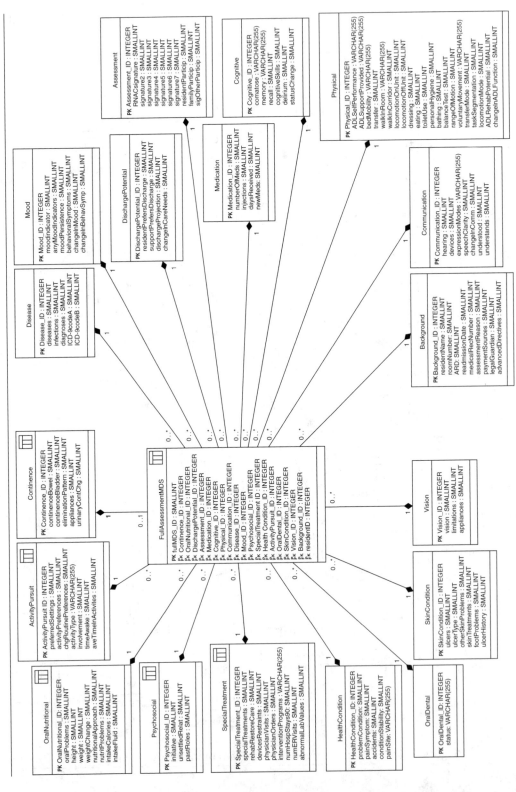

Figure 7–12 Tables that are included only in the Full Assessment MDS

been many foreign keys migrated since each had become a primary and foreign key in the child MDS tables. Using the alternate keys instead of all primary keys means that only one column migrates as a foreign key from the MDS type tables to the MDS table (see Figure 7–13).

The database designers begin to look at the way tables will be queried so that they can include indexes on the tables as needed. There is a lot of information captured in the MDS tables and therefore a lot of data will be required in different queries. The EAB database designers look at each table individually to determine what indexes need to be created. (For this example we look at just the MDS table and uncover the indexes that are needed for it.) The EAB database designers decide to create a few different indexes, one for each of the foreign keys and one composite index that includes both the creationDate and lastUpdate columns (see Figure 7–14). Some databases automatically create indexes for each foreign key, but since EAB has not yet chosen a platform, the database designers include indexes on the model to ensure that the indexes will be created at database generation time.

To ensure that the data collected within the database is correct, the database designers create check constraints on columns and tables. The check constraints are restrictions on the database that are enforced with the implementation of the rule within the constraint. For this example we again focus on only one table, although many tables and columns will have check constraints assigned to them. Since the Resident table has exposure to almost every facet of the database design, we have chosen to work on this table for the example. Some of the constraints can be reused in many different tables as long as the constraints apply to the context. The constraints may be created based on domains that are assigned to the columns within the table, and others are assigned specifically to that column but may be reused on a more global basis.

There are four check constraints on the Resident table: Gender, Birthdate, MedicareResident, and MaritalStatus (see Figure 7–15). Gender is a valid value type of check constraint with the valid values of M or F. Birthdate is a constraint with a rule that enforces that the birthdate must be prior to the admission date. MedicareResident and MaritalStatus are also valid value check constraints. MedicareResident will have the valid Boolean values of Y or N and MaritalStatus values will be M, D, S, or W.

Database Views

Database views are a physical implementation of virtual tables used for reasons including performance and security. The database designers at EAB choose to use views so that they can secure information within certain tables that many different people need to access yet make some of the very secure information

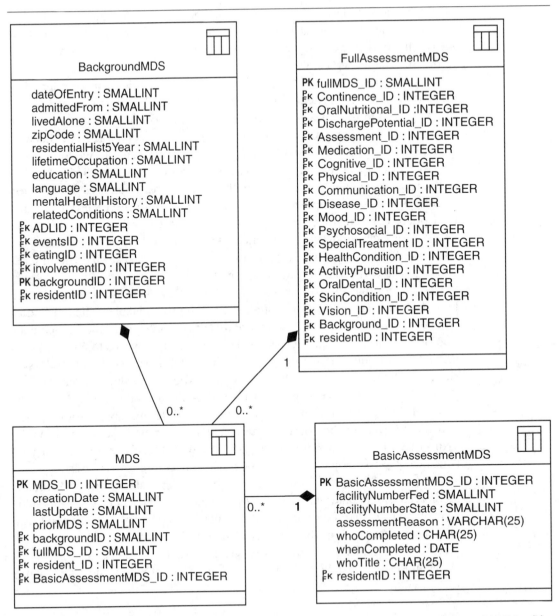

Figure 7–13 Background MDS, Full Assessment MDS, Basic Assessment MDS, and MDS tables showing that only the primary keys have migrated and not the primary/foreign keys

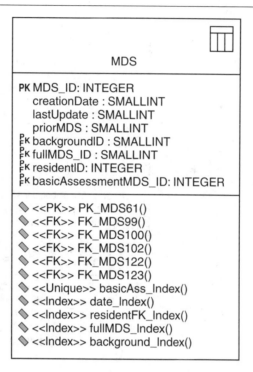

Figure 7–14 MDS table and the new indexes and key constraints

available to only a few people. The other set of views takes information that is often queried from various tables at the same time and puts it together in a view as a virtual table to enhance performance when querying (thus the SELECT statement can query one place and get all needed information). There are many views in the database, but we again focus on only a few.

The view that the EAB database designers start with is on the Resident table and is called the PublicResidentView (see Figure 7-16). This view prevents most users from viewing such information as the patient's social security number, education level, and marital status. There are many groups in EAB Healthcare that do not need this information (and having this information can possibly cause bias toward the patient), so the view excludes these columns. Another view is based on the Background MDS for the information that is needed most often by the accounts receivable team members. They do not need all the information, only some from many tables within the Background MDS and its related tables that supply information for the Background MDS. Therefore, it is much easier and quicker for the application to query one place to get the needed information. This view is called ARBackgroundView (see Figure 7-17).

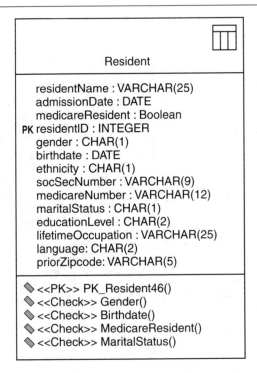

Figure 7–15 Resident table showing columns and constraints

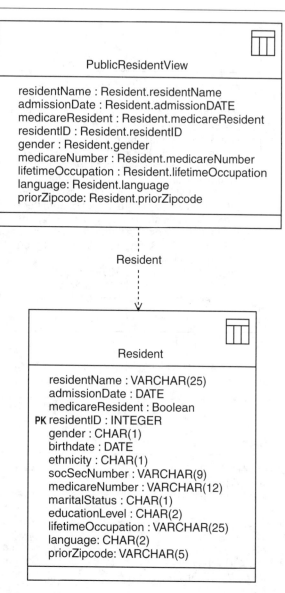

Figure 7–16 PublicResidentView as it is associated to the Resident table

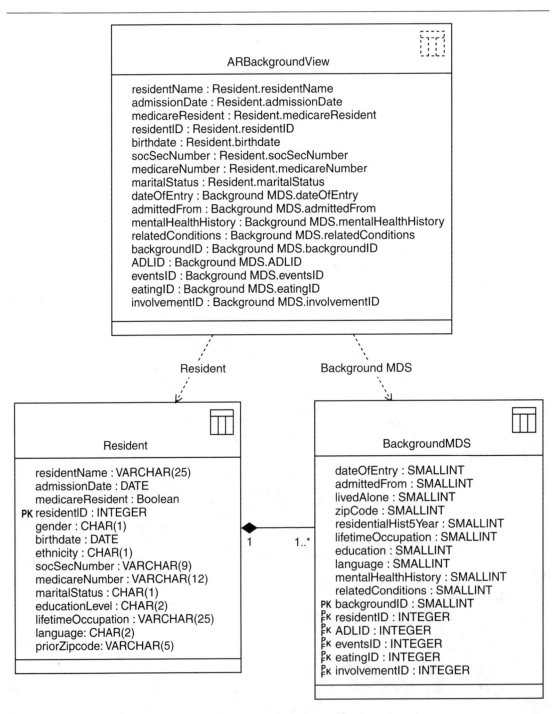

Figure 7–17 ARBackgroundView as it is associated to the Resident and BackgroundMDS tables

Summary

This chapter reviewed the reasons to build a database design, specifically in the UML, and explored in detail the Profile for Database Design created by Rational Software Corporation, although this information is mainly an introduction. The next chapter goes into more detail on the Profile and how to use the UML for deployment and storage of the database elements. The UML has great benefits for database designers: it brings teams together, exposes elements directly on the model that normally get hidden behind modeled elements as tagged values, and describes the database design in great detail. By leveraging work already done in both the requirements and the logical design phases, the database design team at EAB was able to get a quick start on building tables and columns and on understanding the requirements and business reasons for creating the database elements. The constraints needed and ways the database would be used were quite evident because of the work done up front to uncover the needs of people using the database and how it would be used. Using the UML has been quite valuable to all teams so far and now that the database design is based on the logical design. The application developers are working on the application design at the same time based on the same artifacts. When the time comes, it will be more intuitive for the teams to build the object relational mappings and to create the queries of the database.

Chapter 8

Implementing the Physical Aspects of the Database

In this chapter we look at how to implement the database. The design of the database creates many artifacts, but they have to be deployed to a database environment and that takes many decisions of a physical nature. We continue with the modeling process and also get down to the database code, or Structured Query Language (SQL), that needs to be generated to create the database. The modeling aspects of the implementation will focus around the storage of the data. The database designers will look at:

- Database size
- Where the database will reside
  - ◆ Hardware
  - ◆ Software
- Partitioning of the data
- Properties specific to the DBMS chosen
- How the application will communicate with the database

The Workflow

Now it is time for the database designers to start looking at the real physical aspects of the database they have designed. Depending on the development organization, the DBA may get involved or even take over at this point. In some companies, an employee may wear many hats that include both the database designer and DBA, but others may have separate people working on each task. Of course, it depends on your situation, but some teams work together here and others separate this into functions specific to your company's job descriptions. The fact is, it doesn't matter who is responsible for the implementation of the database—it has to get done, and the UML provides the ability to understand quite well what needs to be done to accomplish the job.

Understanding the deployment of the database is very important and can make the difference between continued maintenance and upgrades or a well-running system that lives for a long time. Modeling the storage of the data and how it will be deployed across multiple servers, drives, and partitions enables easy understanding of growth moving forward. Using the requirements that have been captured in the up-front design of the database and systems helps uncover the size of the database and provides information that enables you to estimate growth over time.

As with any other piece of the database design, you can build the database directly with code and not model the database implementation first, but not modeling the database implementation first can cause failure. It is quite difficult to understand textually or by trial and error how the data will lay out, how large the database will be, how quickly the database will grow, and what types and sizes of hardware are needed to support the database system. The database can span many uses and purposes and can grow out of control quickly. Using the UML to model the tablespaces, which tables reside in which tablespaces and how they partition across tablespaces, and which drives contain which tablespaces and where those drives reside are very important tasks and need to be thought out thoroughly and precisely. UML component and deployment diagrams contain the artifacts that can be used to describe each of these functions and graphically display them. By visualizing the deployment and implementation graphically rather than in text, the database designer can easily communicate the layout of the database, see where there are deficiencies, and understand what needs to be done to deal with the issues.

Using Previously Created Modeling Artifacts

The use cases created in the beginning of the project to facilitate understanding of the requirements for building the database system and the various iterations that take place provide a good start for building the database tables, columns, and so on. The use cases also provide a good start for understanding who will be accessing the database and what types of information they will need. Understanding the many users or actors of the system and what types of information they will require gives a good first look into how the database will grow and how quickly.

Activity diagrams are used to describe the flow of user activities in the system and how they interact with the database. There are many tagged values that can be captured on an activity diagram that can help designers understand the frequency of use. Timing of events on an activity can be captured with these tagged values and they can help to again clarify the frequency of accessing the database. The activity diagrams may not drill down onto the specific data that is being accessed, but they give a good high-level view of what data will be captured and how often as well as the activities that lead up to the access of the database.

Sequence diagrams are also used to build the database and application structures by uncovering the objects used in the application and database and turning them into classes and tables. The interaction between objects in the sequence diagrams shows how the objects communicate and through what methods. By understanding how the objects communicate and capturing information on the frequency, database designers can understand the acquisition of data and build indexes. For the deployment of the database, the database designers use the sequence diagrams to understand the frequency of added data to estimate the size of the database and how quickly it will grow over time. Understanding the interactions between objects gives the database designer not only a visual of what is going on between the objects but also the ability to model the frequency of the data access.

The class diagrams help the database designers build a logical design model by capturing the entities, attributes, and associations that are needed to describe the database structure, but they also provide knowledge on how to partition the data. Entities that are persistent generally become tables in the database, but they may be combined into other tables or split into multiple tables. By going back to the logical design model to understand the initial intent of the system, prior to denormalization for the database design, the database designers can understand how application elements or classes may communicate across each other and which data are intended to be accessed by which classes. By understanding the logical design, the database designers can build tablespaces that encompass a user's intent and file the data as a user would access it, rather than just from the abstract of how the database tables are created. Building partitions within a table gives the ability to store parts of the table's data on different drives. A partition may contain different types of data or data based on indexes so that you can store all of the data for customers with names from A to N in one partition and those from O to Z in another partition. Again, by understanding the intent of the system—why it is built and the data that is intended to be stored in the database—the database designers can make highly educated decisions rather than guesses.

With the use of the UML Profile for Database Design designed by Rational Software Corporation, the use of component and deployment diagrams and the artifacts that exist within those diagrams provides a great place to create the elements needed for physical database design, implementation, and deployment. The ability to visualize the physical database information is just one more reason that the UML is the way to design the entire database application from requirements through to the final application and database design. Through the use of modeling artifacts from requirements through to the deployment of the database in one language and modeling technique, rather than some in text, some graphically, and some most likely in code, the database designers can make decisions on the design of the database from one common set of artifacts and be precise in the design of the database architecture.

Putting It All Together

Building the database design starting with requirements and driving through to the completed database implementation is a difficult task, but modeling throughout the entire process can make it much easier to understand. Having all artifacts of the system contained in models and defined in documents for greater detail may seem to be a waste of time, but when you have completed the system and it fits directly with your customer's needs, you will understand that while the modeling process may have taken a little bit longer up front, it saved a lot of time in the end. Having the models for future requirements will help to assess the impacts of changes when the client company needs to upgrade its systems or has realized what items it initially forgot.

The UML has the ability to create separate diagrams, for example, a diagram with the stereotype of <<Use Case>> that contains only elements specific to use cases. You can also break from that plane and not stereotype diagrams so you can include all artifacts needed in one place. Having a diagram that shows a use case and the classes and tables that are created from that use case is helpful for clarifying to both the developers and the end users that the correct information and understanding of the requirements have been met (Figure 8-1).

By creating tablespaces as model elements, you can visualize how tables relate to the tablespaces and where they will reside in the database. With the tables, tablespaces, schemas, and databases on the same diagrams it becomes quite easy to understand how the database is organized. It is important to have the database running at full speed all the time; this can be accomplished by having a well-designed database and taking advantage of specific DBMS properties. Running the database with the correct amount of storage helps keep the database running at its best. It is important to understand what data the database is going to contain, how it will be structured, and how much interaction users will have with the database. By having all of the information captured and

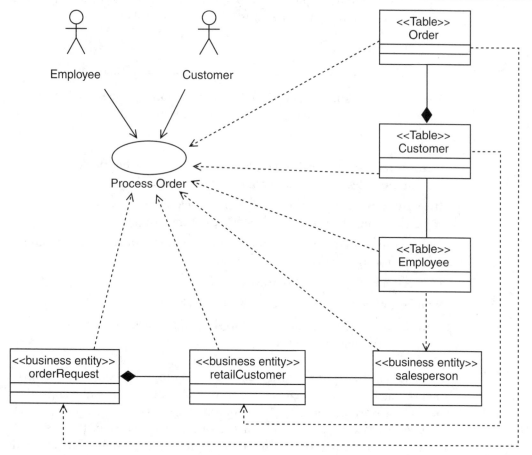

Figure 8–1   Use cases, classes, and tables on the same diagram

designed from the beginning, the database designers can make intelligent decisions when designing the storage of the database.

The Case Study Status

The design of the database is now well under way. The tables, columns, and relationships have been created, the data model has been pretty well denormalized, and it is time to start looking at the physical storage of the data. The EAB Healthcare database designers will work with the database administrators and the system administrators to determine what hardware is available and required, what their specific DBMS requires for storage and its rules, and how to thoroughly capture the data in the best way possible for speed and quality.

The Concepts

The following UML, object-oriented, and other concepts are cited in this chapter. For a more complete discussion and more rigorous definitions of UML concepts, refer to Booch et al. [1999].

Component—a physical and replaceable part of a system that conforms to and provides the realization of a set of interfaces

Dependency—a relationship between two elements in which a change to one element may affect the semantics of the other

Deployment diagram—a diagram depicting the hardware configuration used for the database and applications

Device—a node that has no processing capability

Processor—a node that has processing capability

Connection—the association used to show relationships among devices, processors, and each other

The implementation of the database is accomplished through the development of artifacts that are generated to the database or through script files. To model these artifacts in the UML, components are used. A component is a unit that serves as a building block for the physical structure of the system. The component in database terms serves as a unit that is used for code generation. The components used in database design are tablespaces, databases, and schemas. Components have relationships with other components and with other elements, for example, tables. The relationship used to associate with a component is a dependency. When a dependency exists, for example, between a table and a tablespace, the tablespace's existence depends on the tables involved in the relationship.

Using the UML for database design allows the modelers to model not just database structures but also the deployment or hardware for the system. A deployment diagram has elements available to model such things as the server and its drives. There are two types of elements involved in the deployment diagram: (1) a device, which is a piece of hardware without any computing power, like a drive, and (2) a processor, which is a piece of hardware that can do computation or can be the server itself. Relationships between deployment elements are created using a connection type of relationship.

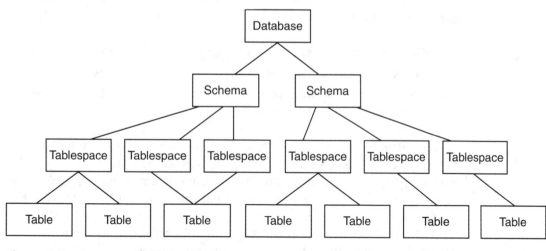

Figure 8–2   Structure of the database storage

Many concepts that are not covered in the UML specifications and books are covered in this chapter as we examine storage modeling from the UML Profile for Database Design. The Profile adds stereotypes and tagged values that are attached to the stereotypes but does not change the underlying metamodel for the UML. This second part of the Profile concentrates on the components and deployment ability of the UML. The structure of the database storage can been seen in Figure 8-2.

The UML Profile for Database Design

As stated many times previously in this book, using the UML to design databases means more than just modeling the database structures of tables, columns, and relationships—it means modeling the entire database design from requirements to deployment. The section of the UML Profile for Database Design that is relevant to this stage of the case study concentrates on the ability to model how and where the data is stored. No matter how many database designers and database administrators we have talked to, when we discuss how to design the storage of the data it always seems to be a difficult subject. The subject of data storage is difficult not because of the technology but because it is hard to understand where everything lies and to ensure that each piece of data is stored in the correct and most economical place. When discussing the UML for database design and its ability to model how the data is stored, we have seen the eyes of database team members just light up. Some of the comments we have heard include

- "This will help me to ensure that I have a storage unit for all data."
- "Now I can see if tablespaces are overused or need to be expanded."
- "It is difficult when partitioning tables to quickly know what data exists where, and modeling would sure help."

We have drawn diagrams all over the world on data storage, and designers in the audience always react the same way: they wish they had this ability in the past and they can't wait to try it. They know it is time consuming to try to understand how to structure the data. Being able to visualize it makes the job much easier.

Using the UML diagram elements available for modeling components gives database designers the ability to model the majority of the storage. Modeling the storage uses

- Components
- Devices
- Dependencies

A component is stereotyped as either <<Tablespace>> or <<Database>> and it assumes additional tagged values based on each. A component is also stereotyped as <<Schema>> and represents the schemas within the database. A device represents a <<Server>> and a dependency is used to draw relationships among the tablespaces, databases, and servers. A dependency is also used to draw a relationship between tables and their assigned tablespaces (Figure 8-3).

There are several attributes that appear on a tablespace as well to capture storage information. A tablespace can be partitioned across several drives and therefore has attributes associated to drives. There can be one or more drives per tablespace. The tablespace also has multiple physical storage volumetric parameters. These parameters are calculations on the size of the tablespace and are captured as tagged values upon the tablespace and often on each individual table. The properties for each tablespace vary greatly depending on the DBMS chosen and even across versions of the same vendor's system. In the Profile, we cover a very generic construct for the tablespace properties, but the UML is extensible, as shown in this chapter, and you can add additional tagged values as needed to accomplish all the modeling needs of your particular DBMS.

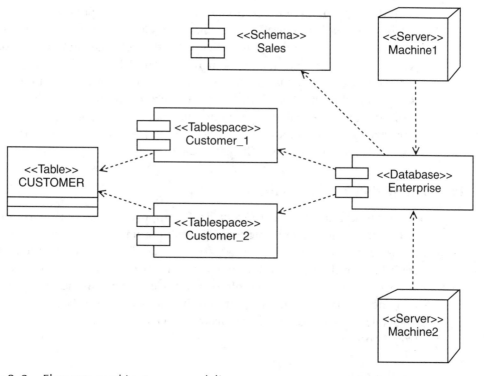

Figure 8–3 Elements used in storage modeling

The Approach

If you haven't already, at this point in the process it is time to choose a specific DBMS vendor. Generally this has been done in advance of building the database design model or at least during that process so that the design can include elements that are useful for the particular server. It is important to have the DBMS chosen by the time deployment is needed so that you have somewhere to deploy the database and so the database design can continue to include the storage.

The database designers work with the database administrators to understand the storage needed for the data. They coordinate their efforts to include the hardware in servers and drives necessary for the data as well as the best way to organize the data into tablespaces and the container to hold it. Tablespaces provide a good way to organize the data to make data easier to find, to prevent data from overloading the server or drives, and to keep similar data together.

As specified in the UML Profile for Database Design, the storage of the data is modeled primarily with components. Using the components to model the database storage for tablespaces, schemas, and databases, the database designers can visualize how the data is to be stored and quickly get an understanding of what data resides where and how much. In the initial steps of modeling the storage, modeling the schema and database may not be so important, but having the tables and tablespaces is. Getting a good representation of how the tables are proportioned across tablespaces and which tables are partitioned into multiple tablespaces is very important for ensuring enough storage room for the data now and as it will grow over the life of the database and application.

Partitioning the Database Tables

Some but not all of the DBMSs available support the ability to partition data within tables across multiple tablespaces or storage units. Some of the databases even allow for partitioning to occur on indexes, including the ability to set values for the index and have different parts partitioned on different tablespaces. An example of partitioning an index is to have an index that includes first and last names. You may partition the index into three parts, for example, one tablespace for names that are from A to G, another from H to R, and the last from S to Z.

Modeling the Schema

A schema is the structure of the database. A database can be made up of multiple schemas. The schema as it describes the database is made up of tables and columns. Since a schema is composed of multiple tables and one or more schemas is used to make up the entire database, it is therefore quite helpful to visualize how tables are related to schemas. Sometimes a diagram becomes quite difficult to read with the many relationship lines it contains, so sometimes it makes sense to leave the relationships off of the diagram but still capture them inside the model as metadata. The schema association to tables can be made late in the game, and often a database is composed of only one schema. It is much more important to build the tablespaces and ensure that they are built properly and allow for proper design.

Modeling the Database

The database itself is modeled as a component, but it is most likely the least important modeling element discussed. When modeling the database, it is comprised of many tables, columns, relationships, tablespaces, schemas, and more, so it is important to understand the database structure and the properties spe-

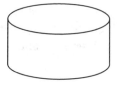

Customer_Transactions

Figure 8–4   Database shown as a cylinder icon

cific to that DBMS as well. The database is modeled as one of the components of the database and is related to tablespaces and schemas through dependency relationships. The database is modeled this way because a database is dependent on the tables that appear in it and on the schema that makes up the database. It does not make much sense to have each individual table have a dependency to the database, and since each table must reside in at least one or more tablespaces, the tablespaces make up the database; therefore, the database has a dependency on the tablespaces. The tablespaces already have a dependency on the tables so, by default, the database will be dependent on the tables as well. As with any modeling element, just because they are captured in metadata does not mean everything must be shown on a particular diagram; some information can be left off for visual purposes. In the UML, a cylinder icon (Figure 8-4) makes it easier to visualize a database on a diagram.

The Design

The database designers at EAB Healthcare have completed the design of the database structures based on the analysis of the requirements for the system and their knowledge of database design. The next step for the team is to figure out the physical structure and deployment of the database—they will design the storage of the data, including where it will reside and how it will be partitioned. The database designers plan to work very closely with the DBAs on this portion of the database design. Designing the storage is where the lines of responsibilities begin to blur a little in EAB's structure, and the teams need a coordinated effort. For the job, we assume that EAB has chosen a relational database vendor for the project. The database will support all of the functionality already supplied by the database design model and will support anything that the storage design calls for. (Rather than selecting a specific vendor for the case study, we choose to remain fairly open and create elements supported by most databases.) The major functionality that the EAB designers come up with that is not supported in all databases is partitioning of tables, although many database vendors seem to be moving in that direction. If you are working on a project for which the chosen DBMS does not support such functionality, you can still use the design techniques described here, leaving out the partitioning.

Creating Tablespaces

Using a component with the stereotype <<Tablespace>> creates a tablespace in the UML, as shown in Figure 8-5. The database designers for EAB first evaluate the tables that exist in the database design to determine what tablespaces are necessary. The designers also take into consideration all of the existing information that has been gathered throughout the entire design process, including the written requirements and all of the diagrams that have been created to describe how EAB Healthcare as a whole will accomplish the creation of the new system.

It is easiest to build tablespaces based on known tables and then to expand them to additional tablespaces, partitioned or combined where needed. The EAB database designers see an obvious place to begin: at the highest level, the MDS itself. The MDS table consists of nine columns, five of which are foreign keys. This table, although consisting of not many columns and therefore few rows, will touch almost every table that exists within the EAB database and at a minimum requires its own tablespace. The database designers create the tablespace called MDS, which is dependent on the MDS table (see Figure 8-6). There are other attribute type values that may be associated with the tablespace, including the drive that contains it, storage size, and minimum and maximum sizes; depending on the database, there can be even more.

The MDS tablespace is a simple example, but the process grows harder as the design continues. Storage modeling is a very iterative process and continues to change even after the database is deployed. Many assumptions have been made, and although they are educated, they are not perfect on the amounts of data that will be captured in the database and how frequently the data will be updated. The database designers are making the first pass at modeling how the storage will be defined. They know they will have to change it somewhat over time. The goal is to make the design as flexible as possible and

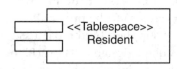

Figure 8–5 Component modeled as a tablespace

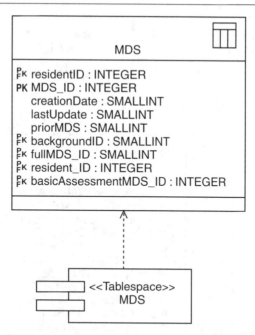

Figure 8–6 MDS tablespace and its dependency on the MDS table

to keep the plans for increasing the number of residents in EAB Healthcare and for expanding the company in the design.

Next the database designers look at the Resident table. Resident is a very large table that contains data for each person who has been a resident at EAB Healthcare—both current residents and ones who have left EAB, by choice or possibly by death. Because of all of the data in the Resident table, the database design team decides to partition the data into three tablespaces, dividing residents into groups according to the first letters of their last names: A to H, I to Q, and R to Z (Figure 8-7). Having the data on different tablespaces enables quicker and easier queries. There are no relationships among residents and this makes the partition easier because the designers do not need to worry about splitting related residents.

The design team continues to look at the highest-level tables and uncovers that there are several different service providers for residents, including Nurse, Internal Care Provider, Therapist, and Dietician. These tables are all assigned to the tablespace ResidentCareProvider (Figure 8-8).

There is another group of workers that takes care of EAB Healthcare overall but doesn't necessarily have direct contact with the residents; they are known as the administrative staff. The administrative staff includes Administrator,

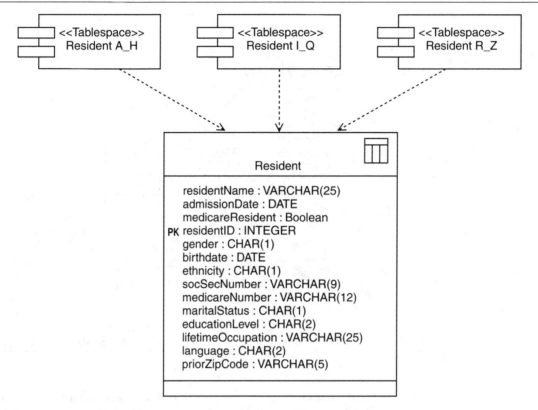

Figure 8–7   Resident table partitioned across three tablespaces

Billing Manager, Medical Records Manager, and Facility Staff. The tables for the administrative staff all belong together since the information that each contains may fall into the other tables' categories and they will often be queried together. The database designers create a new tablespace called Administrative to contain these tables (Figure 8-9).

The database design team follows the flow of packages created in the database design activities to continue with the project. The packages consist of Basic Assessment, Background, and Full Assessment. These three packages make up the remaining tables in the database as created in the database design. The team first looks at Basic Assessment, which is really made up of only one table, BasicAssessmentMDS, and is related to the Resident table. The tablespace is called BasicAssessment and includes just the single table (Figure 8-10).

The Background package gets somewhat more crowded. There are five tables that exist within that package. The tables include InvolvementPatterns,

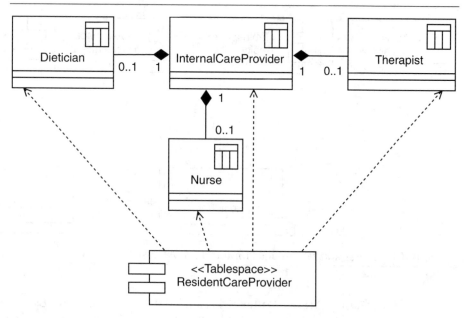

Figure 8–8   ResidentCareProvider tablespace and its dependent tables

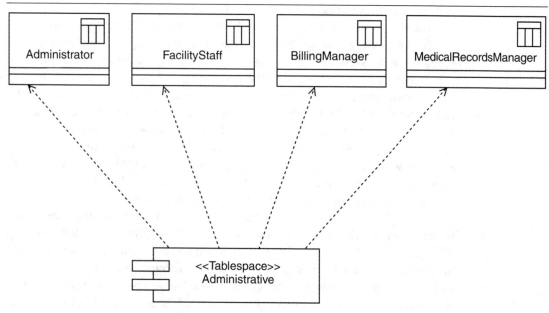

Figure 8–9   Administrative tablespace and its dependent tables

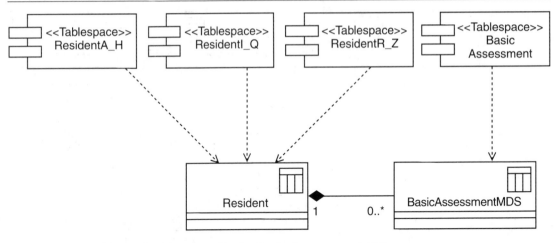

Figure 8–10   Tables and tablespaces for the Basic Assessment MDS

EatingPatterns, DailyEvents, and ADLPatterns plus the BackgroundMDS table which brings it all together. The database designers choose to create two tablespaces for this package, one for BackgroundMDS and one called Background for the other tables (Figure 8-11). The BackgroundMDS table feeds into the MDS table and contains a lot of data within itself along with foreign key references from other tables.

The Full Assessment MDS gets to be quite complex. There are many tables involved and they contain all of the data that make up the Full Assessment MDS. The Full Assessment MDS is the final piece that makes up the entire MDS, which includes the Background MDS and the Basic Assessment MDS. There are 21 different tables with varying amounts of data captured within each table. Using the Establish MDS sequence diagram and others, the EAB database designers take a look back at the way an MDS is established (see Figure 8-12). By understanding who has the input into the MDS, how it is created, and what extent of information is needed for each element within the MDS, the database designers can determine how to arrange the data over tablespaces and assign correct volumetric sizing estimates in creating those tablespaces.

After the intense mining of already captured information and using much of their own knowledge of database design and experiences building several other databases, the database designers make some decisions on how to build the database storage in tablespaces. The team determines that there is a need to have five different tablespaces to represent the Full Assessment MDS. The tablespaces are called FullAssessment (Figure 8-13), MDSSet (Figure 8-14), Physical (Figure 8-15), Treatments (Figure 8-16), and Mental (Figure 8-17).

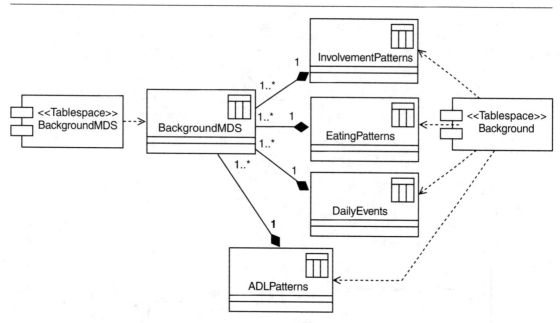

Figure 8–11 Tables and tablespaces for the Background package

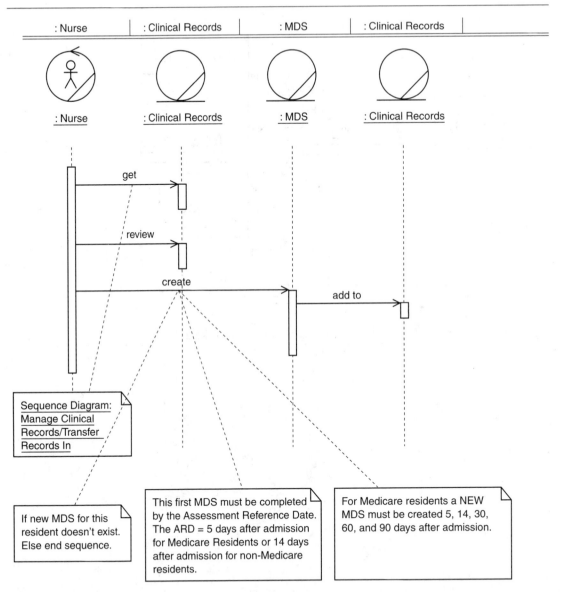

Figure 8–12 Establish MDS sequence diagram used to understand interactions in the creation of the MDS

Figure 8–13 FullAssessment tablespace

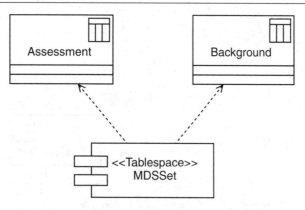

Figure 8–14 MDSSet tablespace

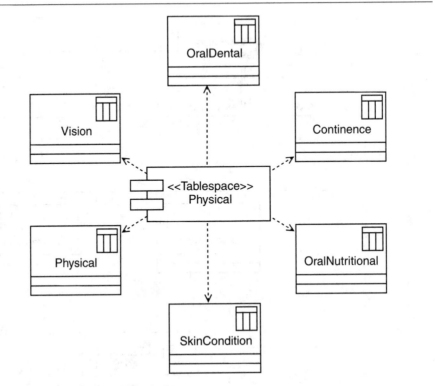

Figure 8–15 Physical tablespace

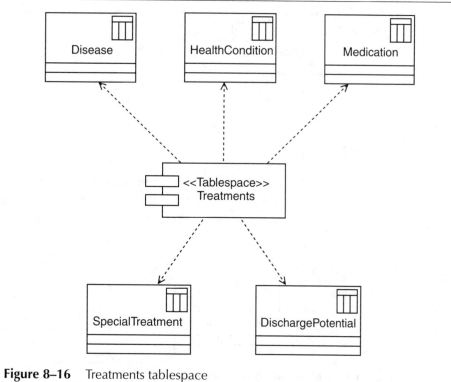

Figure 8–16 Treatments tablespace

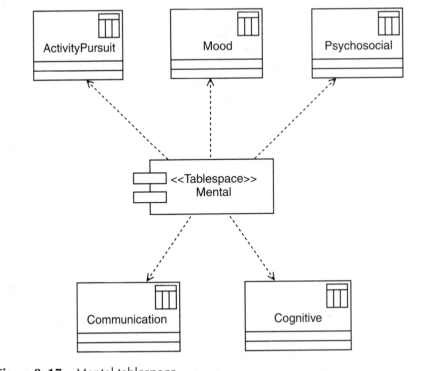

Figure 8–17   Mental tablespace

Determining Schemas and Databases

The database designers have been very busy building all of the tablespaces, setting their properties, and discovering all that is needed in the database storage. The next part is much simpler: they determine the schema and database to which they assign the tables and tablespaces. Since the design of the database is fairly small, they decide to use just one schema and one database and to design the database that way. The schema is called MDSSchema and the database is called MDSDatabase. To model these elements, the designers use components and dependencies to visualize the databases and schemas on the diagram. The database designers build a comprehensive diagram that shows all tables associated to their tablespaces as well as an overview diagram (Figure 8-18) that visualizes the tablespaces and their associations to the schema and database.

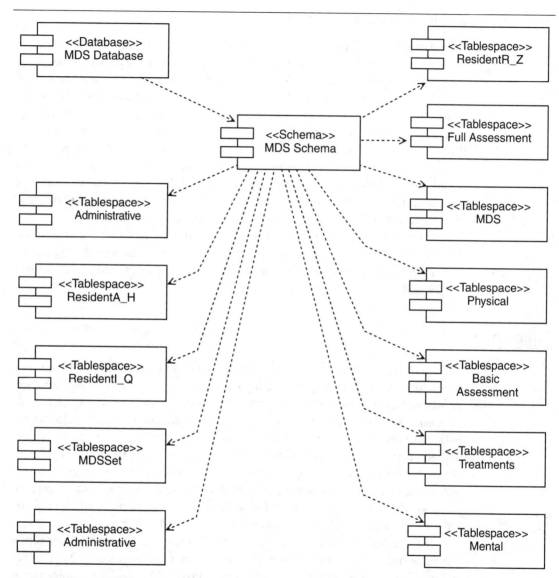

Figure 8–18 Overview of how the tablespaces are related to the schema and database

Designing the Hardware Needed

The database designers at EAB are not hardware experts and don't claim to be, so they give the DBAs and the information technology team the diagrams to help these people visualize what data is being captured. The database designers also provide reports based on those diagrams to explain what the tagged values of the tablespaces include in terms of plans for growth over time. The database designers do not really set up specific diagrams for the others to use, but they give their input so that the information technology team can work its own magic and make the decisions on drives and number of servers needed to build the database correctly. Through use of the UML, the information technology department will continue to add to the diagrams provided by the database designers and will build requirements for the hardware that is needed. They will in turn feed that information back to the database designers to ensure that the technology team correctly understood the diagrams and that the tagged values on the tablespaces are still correct, in case any changes were needed based on the servers and drives available.

Summary

The database designers for EAB Healthcare have had a long, hard job, but they are getting close to completion. They have worked with various development teams, including business and systems analysts, developers, database administrators, end users, and more, to create a well-tuned database design to help run the MDS activities for EAB. They learned some new techniques in capturing and visualizing requirements and for the first time worked together with their development counterparts to design the entire system. As the design and deployment of the system nears the end, the database designers have seen the success of working as a team and modeling all of the relevant artifacts in the database design and not just modeling the tables and columns.

The database design includes how the data will be stored and the properties important to storing the data. The storage modeling uses the UML components and gives the ability to show visually how tables relate to tablespaces, including visualization of partitions, how the tablespaces are associated to the schemas, and the database itself. This has been a great help to the database designers at EAB, giving them immediate feedback on the design of the storage for the MDS database and an easy way to understand what is required and how it can be implemented. Having the ability to model the storage has given the database designers a great form of communication with the database administrators and actually opened the doors to an iterative working relationship. The DBAs were able to give the designers instant feedback on what was needed for the specific database server chosen and how the database designers needed to reorganize the storage as required. If the teams had needed to sift through pages of reports on all of this information, rather than just quickly getting a picture, this process might have taken several more days or even weeks. The entire storage is summed up in just a few diagrams that show how the tables relate to the tablespaces, how the tablespaces relate to the schemas, how the schemas relate to the database, and on what hardware the database will reside.

Chapter 9

Summary of Using the UML
for Database Design

In this chapter we review how EAB Healthcare used the UML to design its database and applications and EAB's results.

The Workflow

The main focus and goal of this book is to provide a practical, usable guide for database professionals that introduces the use of the UML for database design. The design of a database requires a combination of many groups within an organization, including the customer or end user, business analysts, architects, developers, database designers, database administrators, and many more. However, in our case study we have focused on the database design team, which has now begun to see the final results of its hard work.

Although we have shown how the UML can be used for database design, don't get caught up in a panic thinking that there is a new language you now need to learn and that you cannot use the UML for database design until you are an expert in all aspects of it. If you believe that, you will never get going.

Although the UML is a thorough language for complete application and database design, it does not mandate a strict process that must be followed throughout. If you are ready to build the database design but don't know all about the UML, you can start with the logical design or even the database design models and skip the rest. Or you can use information that has already been captured to build these designs.

Although you may not build all of the models, all the project phases should always be covered no matter whether they are modeled or not. For example, the information captured in use cases and activity diagrams needs to be uncovered somewhere and somehow. It may be in a textual document or just in a meeting discussion that leads up to the creation of the logical and database designs. One way or another this is work that must be done if your project is to be successful.

The power of the UML is that it is there for you when you need it, but it is also lightweight enough to get out of the way when you need it to. There are many books that describe various processes of using the UML, but unlike some methodologies, the UML is a flexible language. You can use what you need when you need it and continue moving forward as necessary.

Jump-Starting the Database Design Process

You may recall the process overview shown in Figure 9-1. We used it at the start of the book to show how this book would proceed through the modeling process. Obviously, this is just a slice out of a larger development process that also includes testing and deployment. Let's use this figure to summarize how the database design process can be accelerated, as we have discussed throughout the book. In Figure 9-2 we can see the development artifacts listed that are created very early in the development process (during conceptual modeling). These early artifacts can then prepopulate the subsequent development phases.

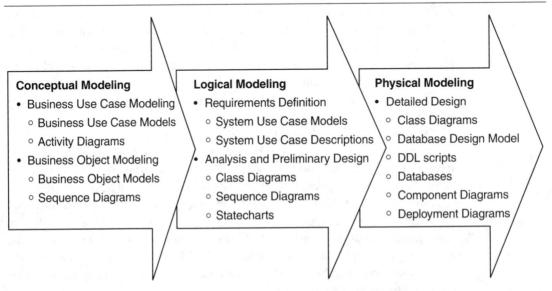

Conceptual Modeling
- Business Use Case Modeling
  - Business Use Case Models
  - Activity Diagrams
- Business Object Modeling
  - Business Object Models
  - Sequence Diagrams

Logical Modeling
- Requirements Definition
  - System Use Case Models
  - System Use Case Descriptions
- Analysis and Preliminary Design
  - Class Diagrams
  - Sequence Diagrams
  - Statecharts

Physical Modeling
- Detailed Design
  - Class Diagrams
  - Database Design Model
  - DDL scripts
  - Databases
  - Component Diagrams
  - Deployment Diagrams

Figure 9-1   Stages of modeling and related UML constructs

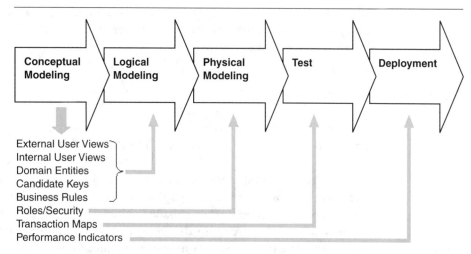

Figure 9–2   Jump-starting the development process by using artifacts yielded early

These artifacts can provide a jump start to your development team and thereby not only accelerate your development but also improve your system quality.

If you have existing legacy artifacts (databases, code, and so on), these too can help jump-start your database design. Why reinvent the wheel when these existing assets can be reverse engineered into your models? (See Figure 9–3.)

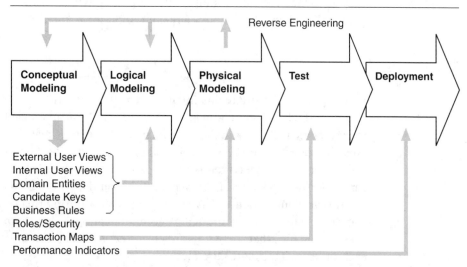

Figure 9–3   Jump-starting the development process by using artifacts yielded early and reverse engineering

Not only does this avoid redundant work, it also provides artifacts that are already operationally proven. Once again, here we have another way to speed development and improve quality.

The Case Study Status

The database designers can take a short breather since they have completed the first designs of the MDS database. The design of the application is an iterative process and the team understands that new requirements are already on the way from the end users just realizing that they missed something initially and from developers needing database changes to accommodate the application. There will also be further enhancements needed on the database for various reasons, new requirements that come in as EAB Healthcare changes its business practices, and changes as the system matures in use.

In the meantime, the database designers are not just sitting around waiting for the next project. Some will move on to other projects, some will begin to look at the existing designs and see where improvements can be made. Perhaps most importantly, some of the database designers will be part of a team, with the other groups involved, to review what they have done. This group will perform a postmortem, which involves looking at the project in detail shortly after it has been completed. The postmortem will look at the project to understand successes and failures, what worked and what didn't in the process and designs. The team will evaluate how the teams worked together, how to better utilize the UML, and how they all came together to build what hopefully will be a successful and useful system that meets the requirements of the business and the end users.

The Approach

It is important for the teams involved with building the complete solution to understand what works and what doesn't so that they can repeat the good and try to correct the bad for future projects. A postmortem is a great way to look back on what has been done on the project shortly after its completion, or sometimes even after moving between project stages, so that the team and management can understand what has been accomplished and how the results were created.

It is very important to have a single mediator during this process. That person makes sure to keep the teams communicating, helps them to bring up issues, makes sure that the issues are clear, keeps teams or people from attacking each other, and facilitates the meeting.

A separate person needs to take notes. It is helpful if the secretary is just an observer, not one of the people involved in the discussions. By not participating

■ **Database Designer**

As you take part in the postmortem process, be sure to include information that would have been helpful for the entire database design but was not available—especially if this is your first time using the UML to create a collaborative development effort, since you will not get it 100 percent right the first time. Be sure to take part in the entire process; participate more than just when the database design models themselves are discussed. Remember that the entire modeling design process can be used not just for the application development and analysis but also for requirements definition and the development of the database itself. If there is additional information that could have been captured early but was not, include that in the issues list to be accomplished next time. If the use cases, for example, need more detail as to how the data will be captured (for example, via the Internet, external sources, or just employees), this can be added to the requirements documentation or even to metadata descriptions captured directly against the use case itself. Are there additional extensions that you as a database designer need to make to the UML to better do your job? Get them on the list as well. Maybe your organization has some special policies or standards that you apply to the database. There can be additional tagged values or stereotypes created and used in that circumstance. Don't forget, this activity should capture both positive and negative items. So include what didn't work and what worked well. You may not be involved directly in the next project, but the next group will benefit from using your knowledge of what you learned and what helped make the project a success.

in the discussion itself, the secretary can take notes without the distractions of involvement, making sure to track everything and not putting any personal opinions into the notes.

The Design

A good-sized group of people involved in the development effort for EAB Healthcare has come together off-site for a day to look at the job they have just accomplished. The group is composed of some development managers, analysts, developers, and database designers. The Chief Technology Officer and the Vice President of Information Technology have also joined the meeting to understand how this unique project has been done. For the first time at EAB, an entire development team has worked together to create an application and database, including gathering the requirements all as one group, rather than in individual teams. Management wants to understand the benefits and issues and learn how they can make this process a continued success moving forward.

The group contributing to the postmortem is limited to three people from each involved development team. If too many people are involved, it is difficult to get much accomplished and to give everyone enough time to present their views. The people participating in the postmortem were selected by the team leader of each group involved; the team leaders attend the postmortem as well. Each team includes both senior- and junior-level people, giving insights from all aspects of the project.

For a few days prior to this meeting, the representatives spent time gathering information from their teams as input into the meeting and they are now ready to present their findings. The facilitator for the meeting is the Director of Information Research and Development. Although she was involved somewhat in the process, she is still outside the day-to-day activities enough to be a good facilitator. She can also understand the conversations to be sure that they are resolved to their fullest. Part of the facilitator's job is to put time limits on conversations and to make sure that they stay on the subject. There is a large clock on the wall, and the facilitator directs that no one issue can be discussed for more than five minutes. This could potentially limit the input, but it will help control the group from drilling too deep into a subject and thus getting off track.

The meeting starts off with a demonstration of the MDS application and how it interfaces with the database that was created. This gives everyone the satisfaction of seeing the first phase of the project complete and a great positive attitude for a starting point. It is important that the team members not have negative attitudes coming into the meeting but also not to be so positive that they are blind to real issues.

The Positives

The overall attitude of the development team at EAB is quite positive. This was the first time that all of the teams involved in the development of a project were able to work together and build the entire system from a single set of artifacts. The database team is really impressed with the requirements that they were able to share across the different teams involved. The team members have never had such a clear set of requirements nor such a clear definition of artifacts to build the database. In most past projects, the database team was used to getting the requirements and systems definitions on its own, and they often contradicted what the other teams had created. Models of the requirements in use cases and the activities that defined those use cases were unheard of previously. The team members had built some business and business process models in the past, but never anything like this. The ability to have many tables defined prior to even starting the database design models amazed the database team. This is not to say that they didn't capture requirements and didn't do their background work, but they think it's great to have one single set of artifacts.

The database designers are happy they used the UML for the database design models themselves. They found it very easy to learn the notation and understand the relationship types. The database designers also found the most useful parts of using the UML were the ability to visualize so many artifacts, including the constraints, triggers, and stored procedures. The biggest benefit they see in using the UML is the ability to model the tablespaces and quickly understand what tablespaces exist and how tables are partitioned across those tablespaces. During the design process, it was great to visually see what already existed and where new items needed to be created.

The analysts see some benefits to their new method of modeling as well. They have been using the UML for two years and they already understood its benefits at the start of the EAB project. However, they had never before been able to communicate their designs to so many people in one language. During the postmortem, the analysts present their view: "Creating the conceptual and logical designs together with the rest of the organization was a great help. This was the first time we have developed an application with an understanding of the requirements throughout the process of design." The analyst group was able to work with everybody to define requirements together, causing a much better understanding of the system and enabling the building of a comprehensive design from requirements to application to the final database.

The application developers are also impressed with the use of the UML for everyone involved. Like the analysts, the developers had used the UML before this project, but the developers had only about six months of experience and had never really been too involved with the early requirements work. The developers are now quite happy that they were involved so early for the EAB job. During the process they really felt that they had decision power in creating the application and defining the requirements, instead of being handed the prototypes with the onus to "build this." The other major benefit the developers see is the ability to communicate with the database designers. In the past, developers had to beg to see the database designs and then, well, good luck trying to figure out how the tables and classes map. Having the entire design in one language broke down the barriers to communication. Mapping to basically one metamodel gave them the ability to understand the object relational mapping and build a solid system.

The Negatives

When you have positives, of course there are going to be negatives as well, especially with such a drastic change in philosophies. The development teams had never really worked together in one language to build a system. They had obviously worked on projects that interfaced with each other, since the application and database must communicate, but the teams' communications were never good. Issues arise whenever you throw something new into the mix. Having a new language and methodology and the need for the teams to work so closely together opened the project up with a lot of concerns. Change, although often for the better, is not usually conceived as such initially, and these teams were no different.

The group that took the change the hardest was the database designers. Although they have been modeling much longer than the others, the notation and language was completely foreign to them. They feared that having the developers and analysts involved in the database design would just cause delays with nobody getting anything accomplished. Most of these issues were overcome quickly, but still they created a negative expectation in the beginning. Also, few tools were available to support the entire process, and a decent amount of manual work had to be done. Although the team members believe this will improve with time, at the postmortem they present this as a negative. All the teams report that, although they began to work together, each still has a feeling of "we know our piece of the system best and don't question us." This is something that, over time, will change as each group develops more subject matter experts in analysis and design across the project life cycle.

The analysts bring up some issues about the database designers not listening to them early in the project. They feel that the database designers were thinking of everything in a data perspective and didn't think outside of their box. This is something that the team members will have to work to overcome. Since this is so new to them, it is quite difficult. Even though one has the company's best interest in mind, one still may be thinking of oneself, and it is difficult to get away from that.

The application developers are of the same opinion as everyone else. They see the many benefits of using the UML, but the process still isn't perfect and there is plenty of room for improvement. The developers want to be more application centric. It wasn't quite as easy as expected to map from the logical design to the application design while still keeping the object relational mapping intact. During the process they saw that some of the logical design models began to become just logical data models, and that was not what they expected out of a logical design. They now see a need for the database designers to step back a little from the database world and just think of the logical design from a nonpartial point of view.

The application developers also, as everyone in the group does, want more. They want to see more of the application logic captured in the model designs and to have more of that code generated automatically from a model by some tool set. Most tools only generate the class code, leaving the business logic to the developers themselves. The developers see an advantage of keeping the logic directly in the model and modeling the business logic itself, helping to keep the model and code synchronized. This would keep the models complete with all artifacts needed for development.

Summary

Overall, the project has been very successful. For the first time ever at EAB Healthcare all of the parties involved with the development process were able to work together to solve a business problem. It was great to have the team work together from start to finish while allowing individual groups to take over, where needed, in their own subject matter areas, such as the database designers building the database design. Using one language and notation made it easy for the teams to communicate, and the developers saw the biggest advantage in building the database queries needed by the application. The database designers saw that change can be good, and they picked up some valuable information from the common requirements. Also, by changing to a new modeling language they can now quickly understand and visualize more database elements than ever before. The analysts were able to get input into their designs from every party involved that would be using them. That made the requirements true to life. The requirements were not just artifacts that would never be examined but elements of the design used by everyone involved. The teams eagerly look forward to using their newly developed UML skills on their next project.

Appendix A

UML Models for EAB Healthcare, Inc.

This appendix contains various models and diagrams that provide more complete information on the project discussed in the EAB Healthcare case study. Some have been referenced in the previous text and some have not.

Organization of This Appendix

The models and diagrams are grouped according to six main types: business use case models, business object models, traditional conceptual data models, system use case models, design models, and database design models. This appendix is further organized as detailed below.

The Business Use Case Models

- Global view of Provide Resident Care business use case
- Overview of Provide Resident Care business use case
  - Accounts Receivable business use case
    - Billing activity diagram
    - Reimbursement activity diagram
  - Comply with Regulations business use case
    - Compliance Assessment activity diagram
    - Compliance Review activity diagram
  - Manage Clinical Records business use case
    - Transfer Records activity diagram

- Provide Clinical Care business use case
  - Provide Clinical Care activity diagram
- Respond to Inquiry business use case
  - Respond to Inquiry activity diagram

The Business Object Models

- Accounts Receivable business use case
  - Accounts Receivable business object model
    - Evaluate Eligibility sequence diagram
    - Submit Invoice sequence diagram
    - Verify Reimbursement sequence diagram
- Comply with Regulations business use case
  - Comply with Regulations business object model
    - MDS view
    - Nurse view
    - All actors view
    - Accreditation sequence diagram
    - Establish MDS sequence diagram
    - Investigate Concerns sequence diagram
      - Investigate Concerns: Invalid sequence diagram
      - Investigate Concerns: Valid sequence diagram
    - Maintain MDS sequence diagram
    - Review Compliance sequence diagram
    - Transmit MDS sequence diagram
- Manage Clinical Records business use case
  - Manage Clinical Records business object model
    - Medical Records Manager view
    - Transfer Records In sequence diagram
    - Admit Prior Resident sequence diagram
    - Transfer Records Out sequence diagram
    - Close Records sequence diagram
    - Destroy Records sequence diagram
- Provide Clinical Care business use case
  - Provide Clinical Care business object model
  - Update Care Plan business object model
    - All actor view
    - Establish Treatment sequence diagram
    - Update Treatment: Physician sequence diagram
    - Update Treatment: Medical Supply Vendor sequence diagram
    - Update Treatment: Other sequence diagram
    - Establish Care Plan sequence diagram

- Update Care Plan sequence diagram
- Provide Services sequence diagram
■ Respond to Inquiry business use case
  ◆ Respond to Inquiry business object model
    - Respond to Inquiry sequence diagram

The Traditional Conceptual Data Models

■ Clinical Records data model

■ Schedules and Reports data models

■ Miscellaneous data models

The System Use Case Models

■ Actors
  ◆ Auditors and agents
  ◆ Care providers
  ◆ Other actors

■ Use cases
  ◆ Comply with Regulations use case diagram
  ◆ Manage Clinical Records use case diagram
  ◆ Provide Clinical Care use case diagram

The Design Models

■ Comply with Regulations business use case realization
  ◆ Comply with Regulations class diagram
  ◆ Establish MDS use case realization
    - Establish MDS class diagram
      • Establish MDS sequence diagram
    - Nurse view class diagram
  ◆ Maintain MDS use case realization
    - Maintain MDS sequence diagram
  ◆ MDS Definition
    - MDS structure overview class diagram
    - MDS high-change elements class diagram
    - MDS medium-change elements class diagram
    - MDS low-change elements class diagram
  ◆ Transmit MDS use case realization
    - Transmit MDS class diagram (initial)
      • Transmit MDS sequence diagram
    - Transmit MDS class diagram (revised)

- Included use cases
  - ◆ Security Access use case realization
    - – Security Access class diagram
    - – Access Clinical Records sequence diagram
    - – Verify Security sequence diagram

The Database Design Models

- Comply with Regulations business use case realization
  - ◆ Comply with Regulations database diagram
  - ◆ Establish MDS use case realization
    - – Establish MDS database diagram
    - – Nurse view database diagram
  - ◆ MDS Definition
    - – MDS structure overview database diagram
    - – MDS high-change elements database diagram
    - – MDS medium-change elements database diagram
    - – MDS low-change elements database diagram
  - ◆ Transmit MDS database diagram

The Models and Diagrams

The Business Use Case Models

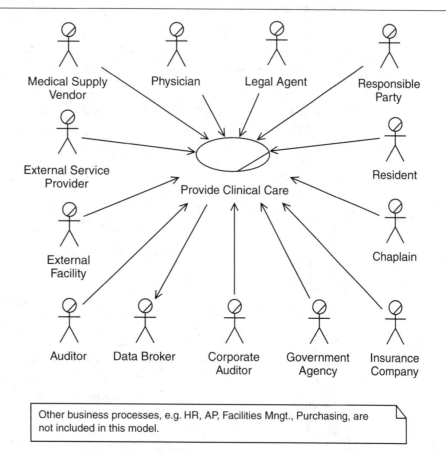

Medical Supply Vendor

Physician

Legal Agent

Responsible Party

External Service Provider

Resident

Provide Clinical Care

External Facility

Chaplain

Auditor Data Broker Corporate Auditor Government Agency Insurance Company

Other business processes, e.g. HR, AP, Facilities Mngt., Purchasing, are not included in this model.

Figure A–1 Global view of Provide Resident Care business use case

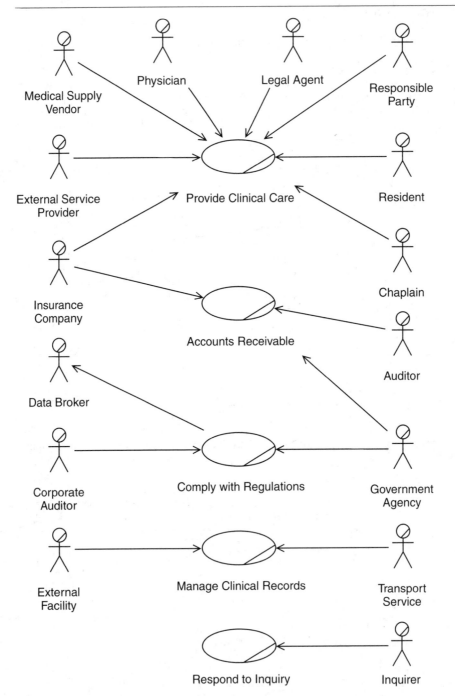

Figure A–2   Overview of Provide Resident Care business use case

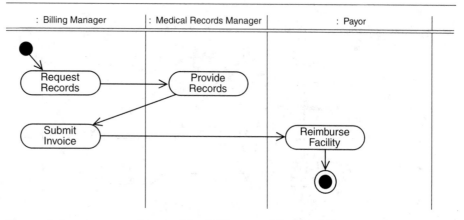

Figure A–3   Accounts Receivable, Billing activity diagram

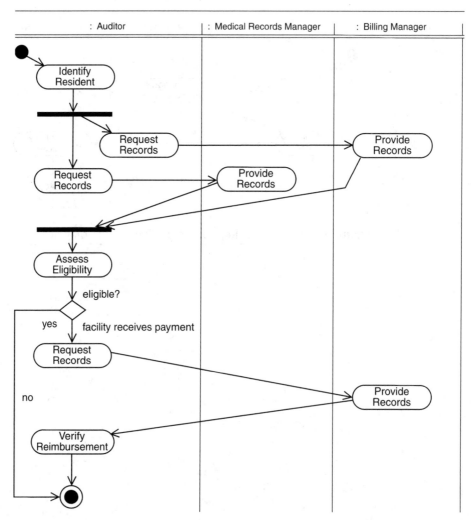

Figure A–4   Accounts Receivable, Reimbursement activity diagram

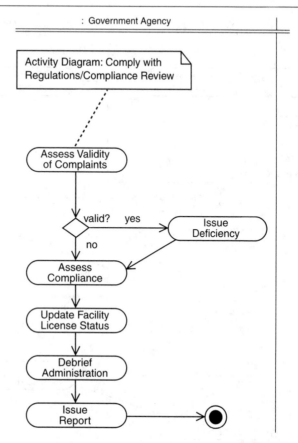

Figure A–5   Comply with Regulations, Compliance Assessment activity diagram

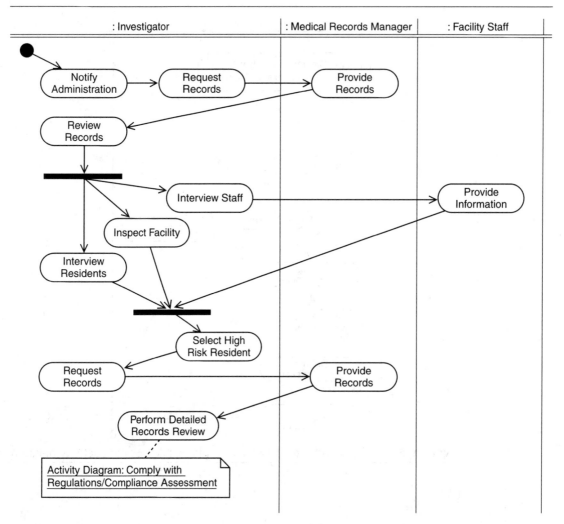

Figure A–6 Comply with Regulations, Compliance Review activity diagram

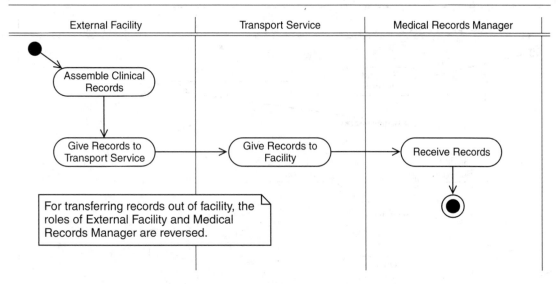

| External Facility | Transport Service | Medical Records Manager |

Figure A–7   Manage Clinical Records, Transfer Records activity diagram

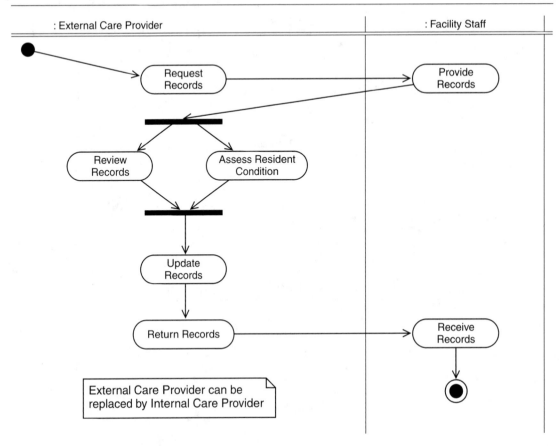

Figure A–8   Provide Clinical Care activity diagram

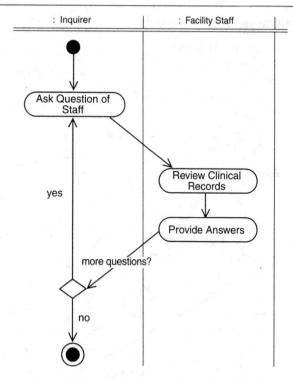

Figure A–9   Respond to Inquiry activity diagram

The Business Object Models

Accounts Receivable

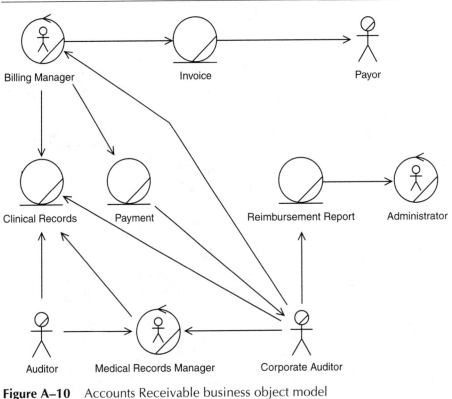

Figure A–10   Accounts Receivable business object model

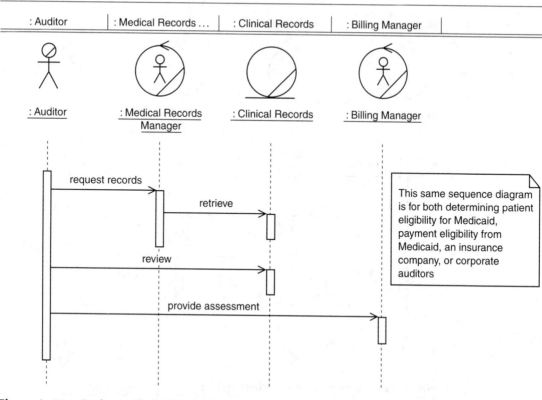

Figure A–11 Evaluate Eligibility sequence diagram

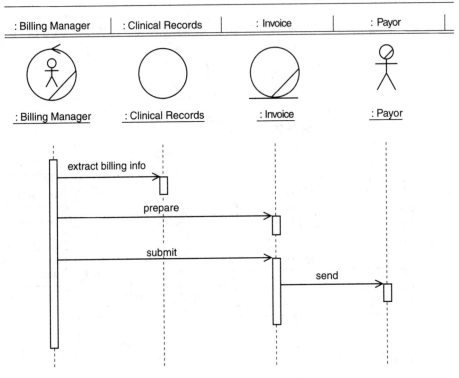

Figure A–12   Submit Invoice sequence diagram

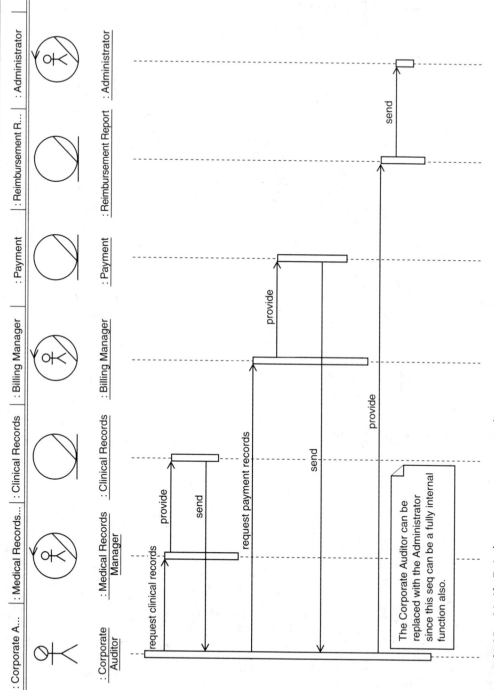

Figure A–13 Verify Reimbursement sequence diagram

Comply with Regulations

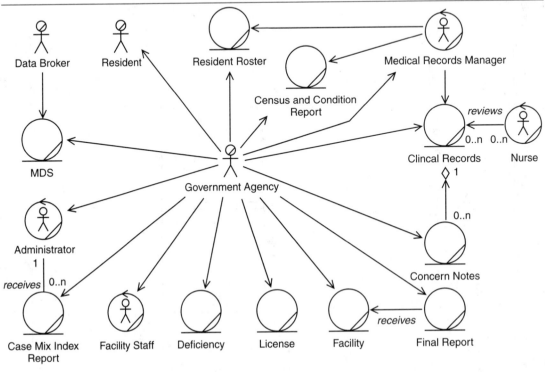

Figure A–14 Comply with Regulations business object model

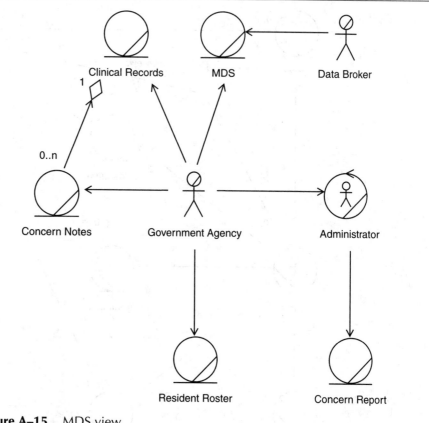

Figure A–15   MDS view

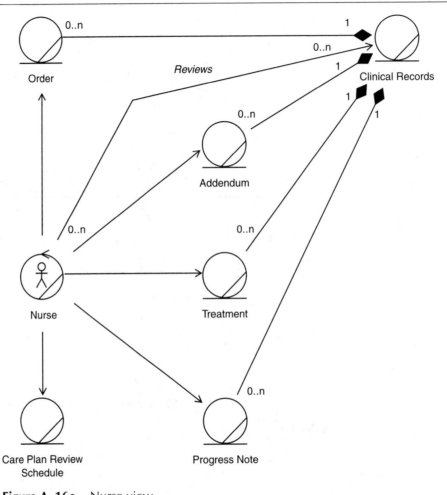

Figure A–16a Nurse view

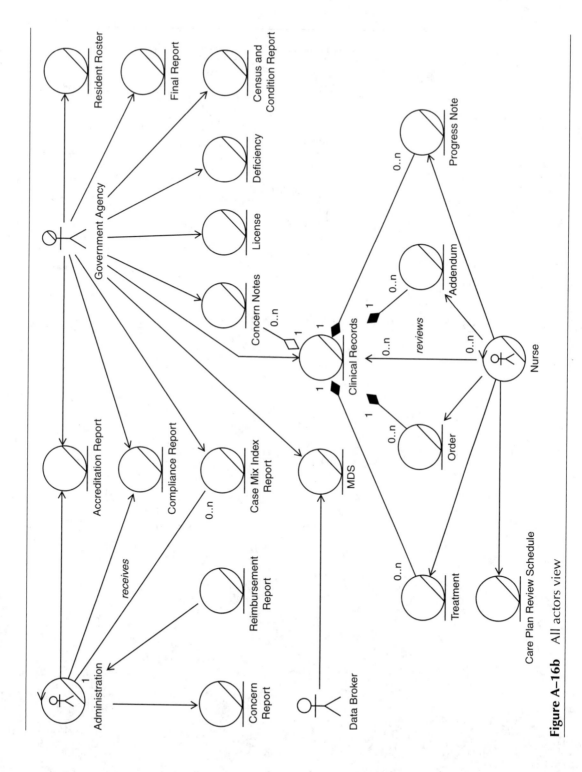

Figure A–16b All actors view

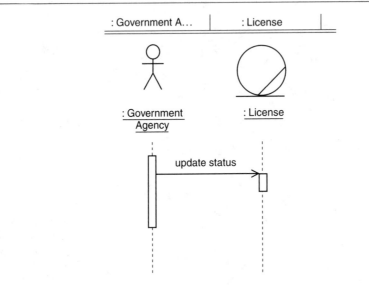

Figure A–17   Accreditation sequence diagram

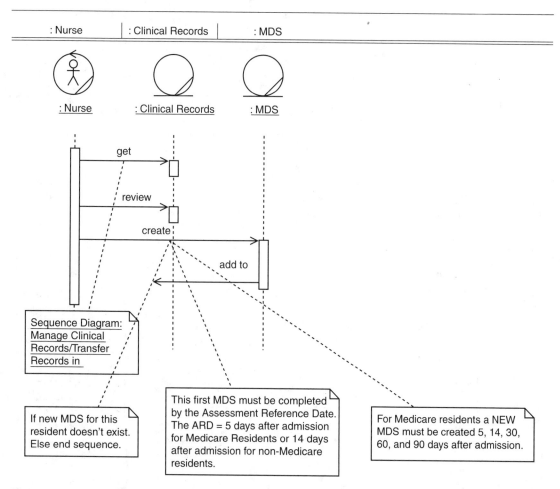

Figure A–18   Establish MDS sequence diagram

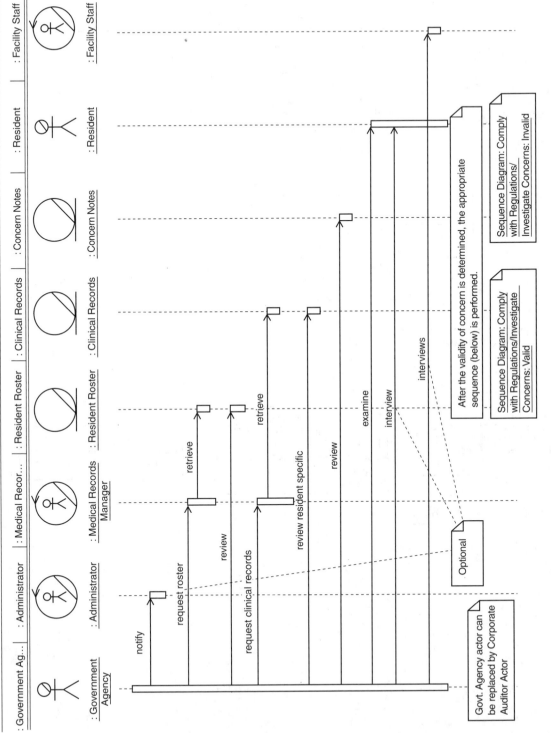

Figure A–19 Investigate Concerns sequence diagram

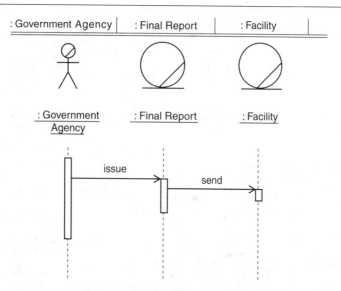

Figure A–20 Investigate Concerns: Invalid sequence diagram

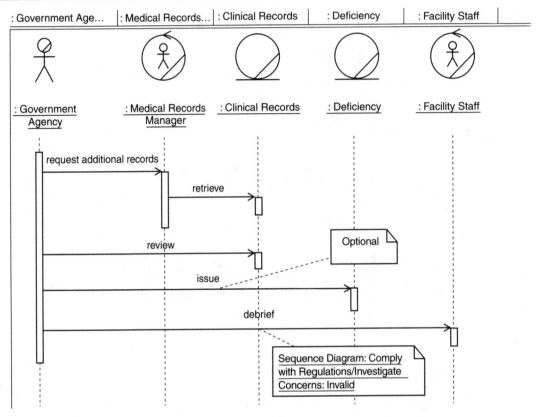

Figure A–21 Investigate Concerns: Valid sequence diagram

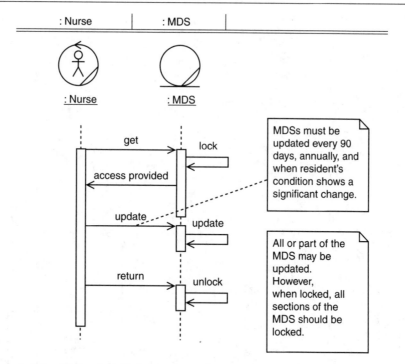

Figure A–22   Maintain MDS sequence diagram

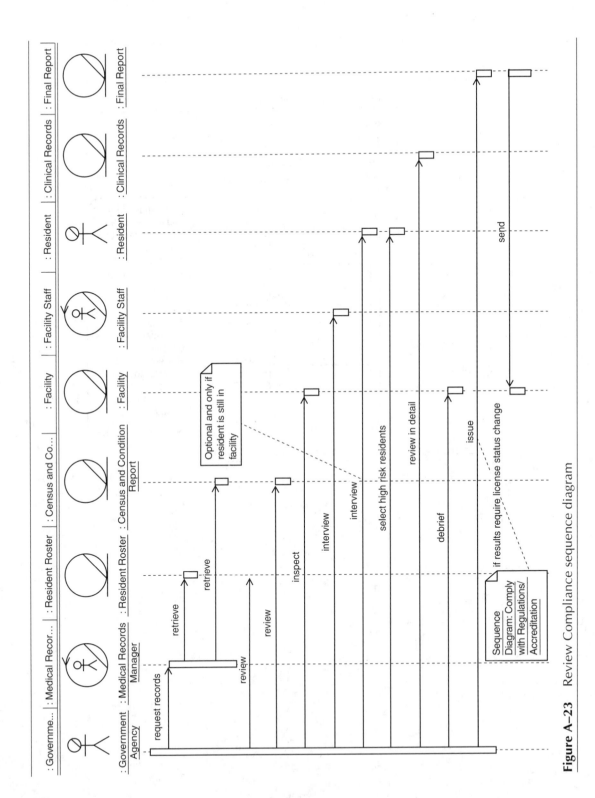

Figure A–23 Review Compliance sequence diagram

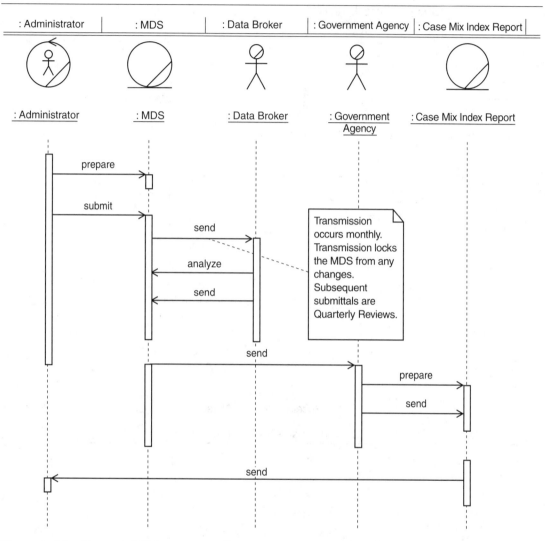

Figure A–24   Transmit MDS sequence diagram

Manage Clinical Records

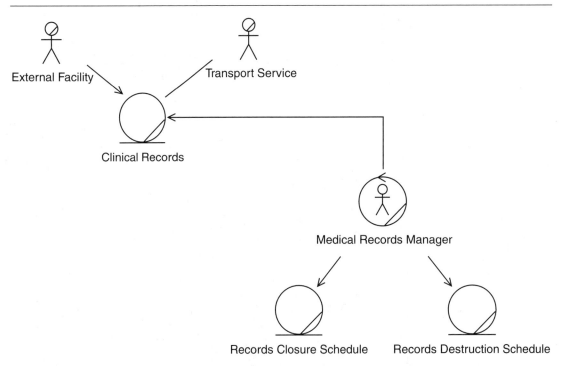

Figure A–25a Manage Clinical Records business object model, Part 1

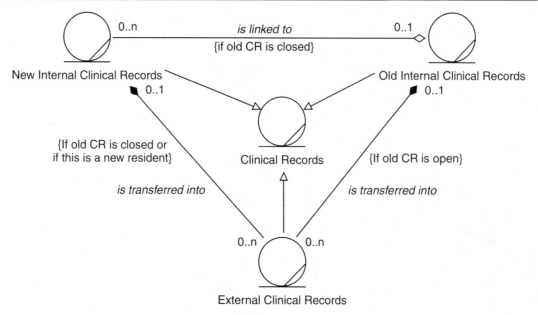

Figure A–25b   Manage Clinical Records business object model, Part 2

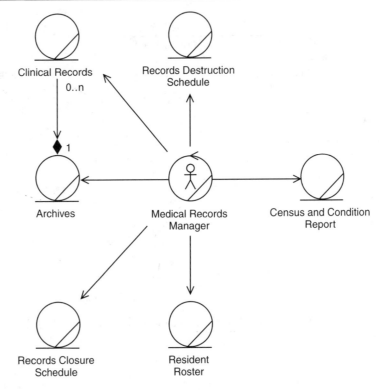

Figure A–26 Medical Records Manager view

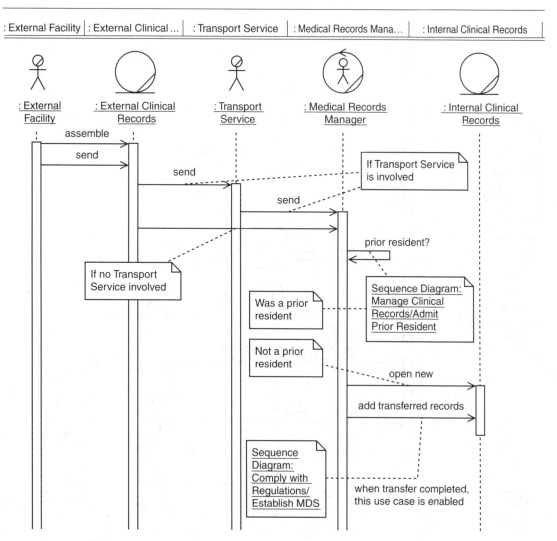

| : External Facility | : External Clinical ... | : Transport Service | : Medical Records Mana... | : Internal Clinical Records |

Figure A–27 Transfer Records In sequence diagram

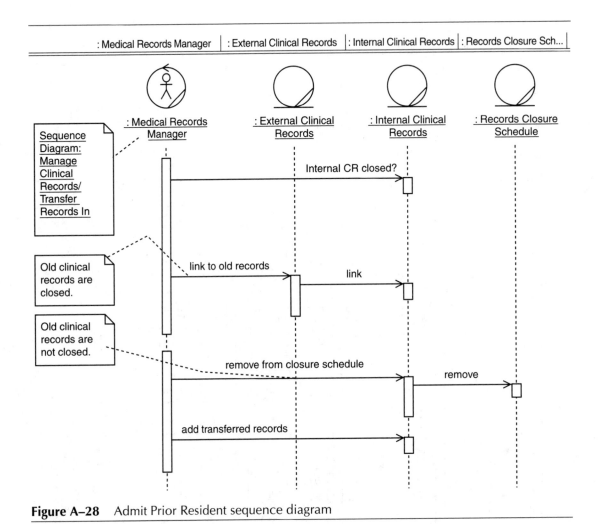

Figure A–28 Admit Prior Resident sequence diagram

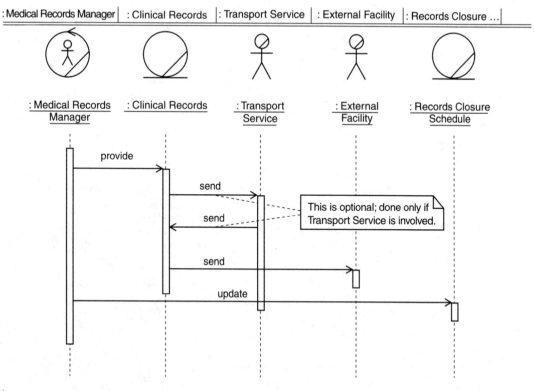

Figure A–29   Transfer Records Out sequence diagram

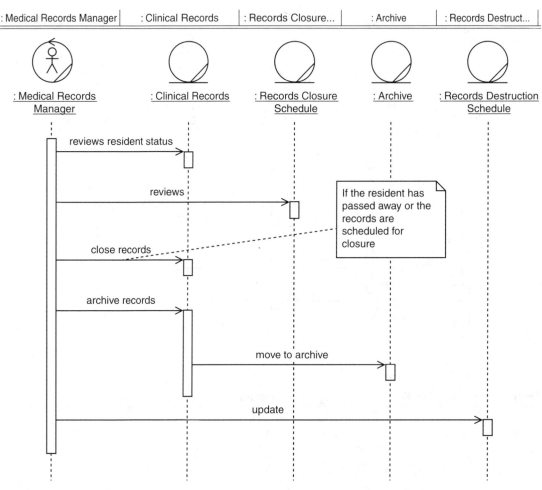

Figure A–30 Close Records sequence diagram

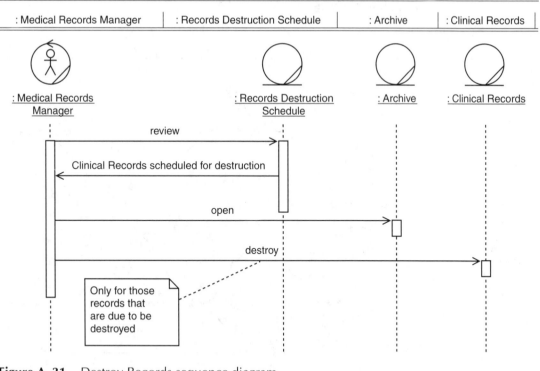

| : Medical Records Manager | : Records Destruction Schedule | : Archive | : Clinical Records |

Figure A–31   Destroy Records sequence diagram

Provide Clinical Care

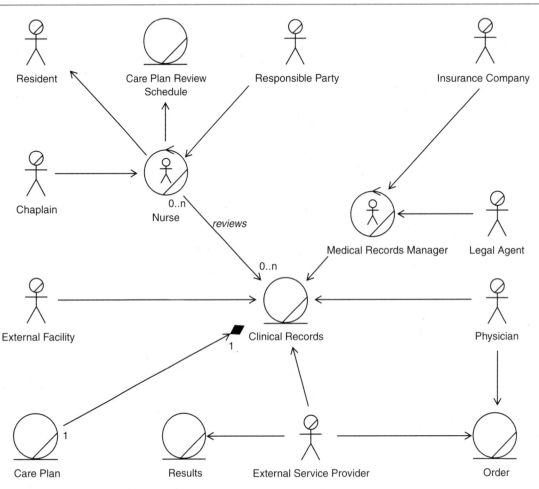

Figure A–32 Provide Clinical Care business object model

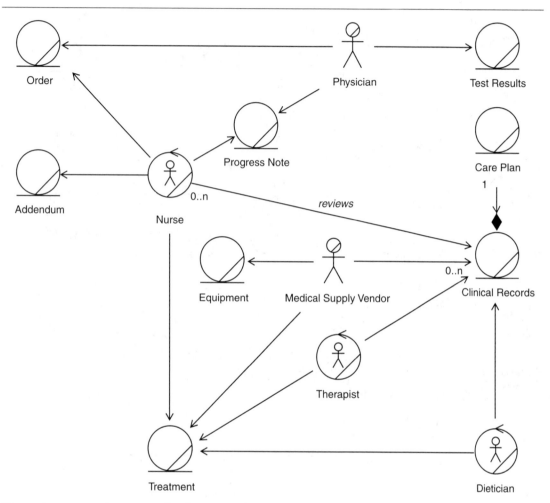

Figure A–33 Update Care Plan business object model

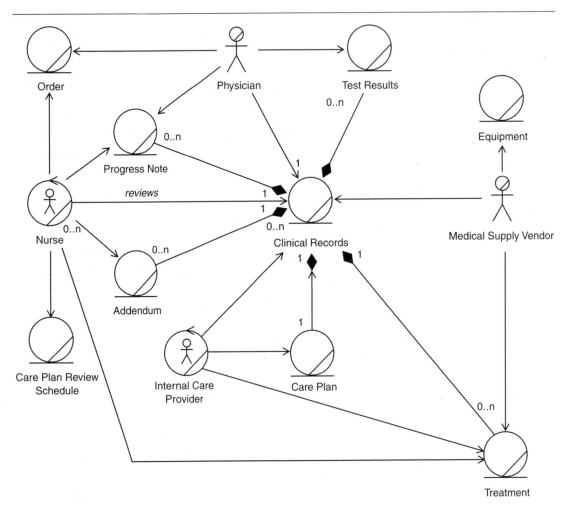

Figure A–34   All actors view

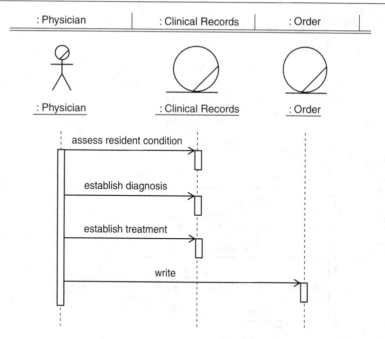

Figure A–35   Establish Treatment sequence diagram

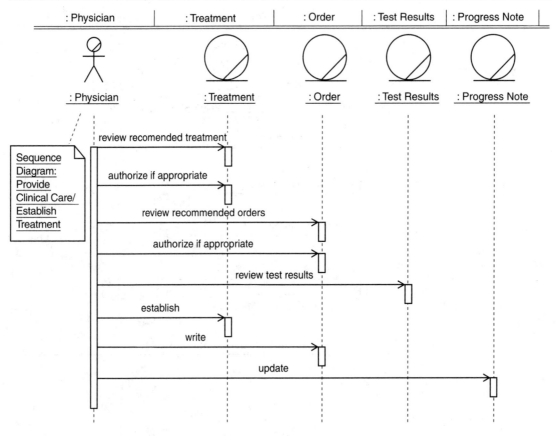

Figure A–36 Update Treatment: Physician sequence diagram

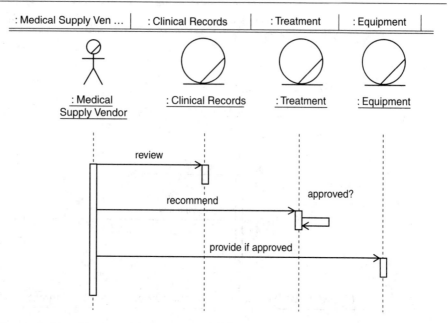

Figure A–37   Update Treatment: Medical Supply Vendor sequence diagram

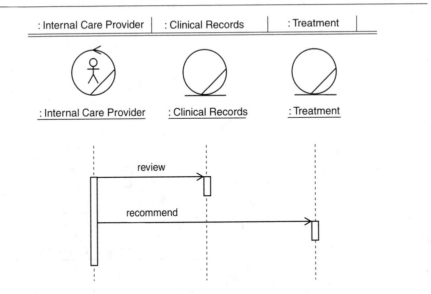

Figure A–38   Update Treatment: Other sequence diagram

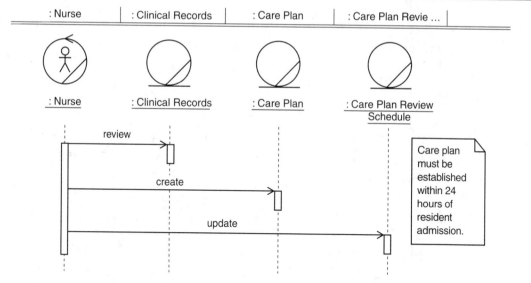

Figure A–39   Establish Care Plan sequence diagram

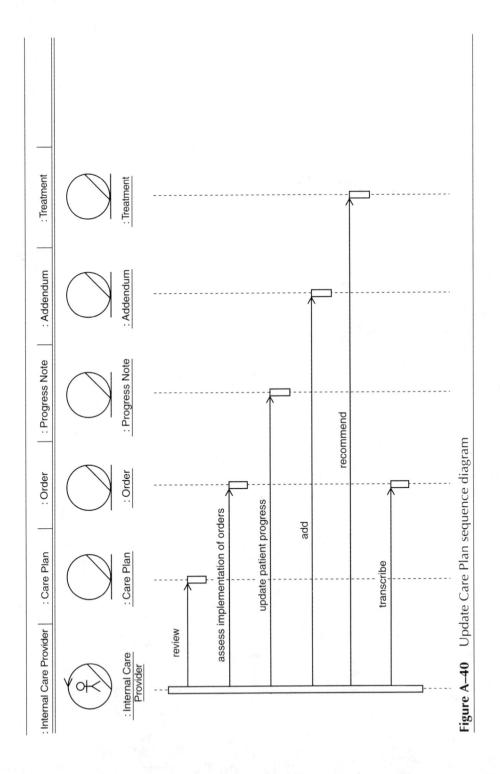

Figure A–40 Update Care Plan sequence diagram

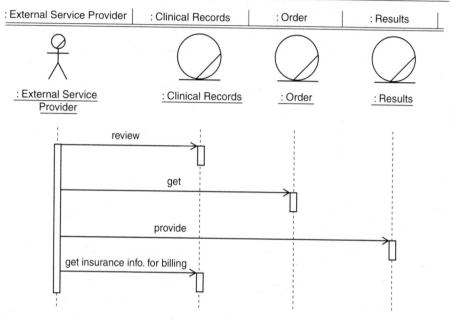

Figure A–41 Provide Services sequence diagram

Respond to Inquiry

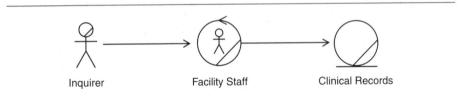

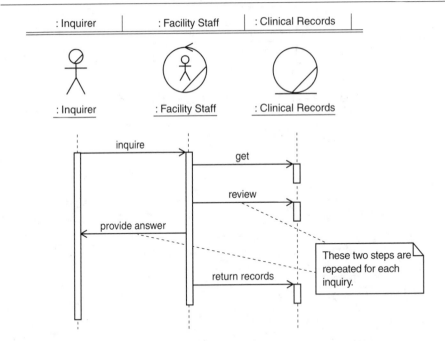

Figure A–42 Respond to Inquiry business object model

Figure A–43 Respond to Inquiry sequence diagram

The Traditional Conceptual Data Models

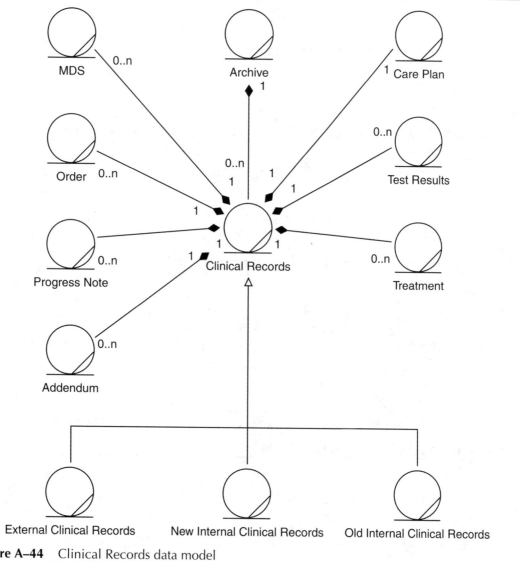

Figure A–44   Clinical Records data model

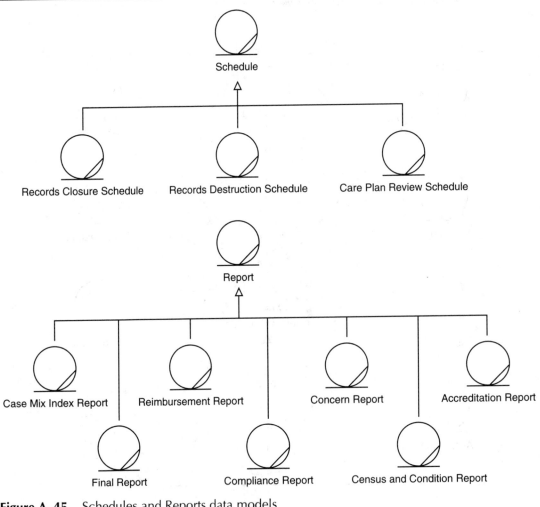

Figure A–45   Schedules and Reports data models

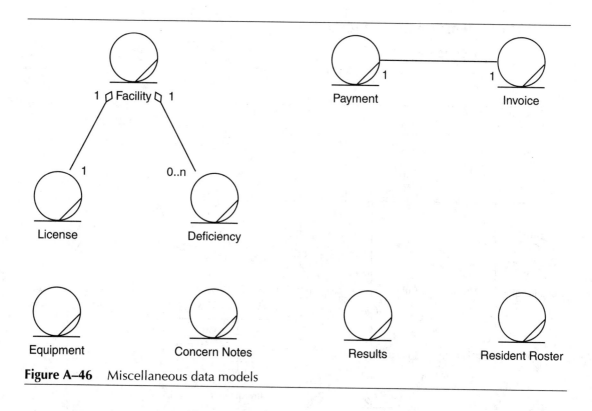

Figure A–46   Miscellaneous data models

The System Use Case Models

Actors

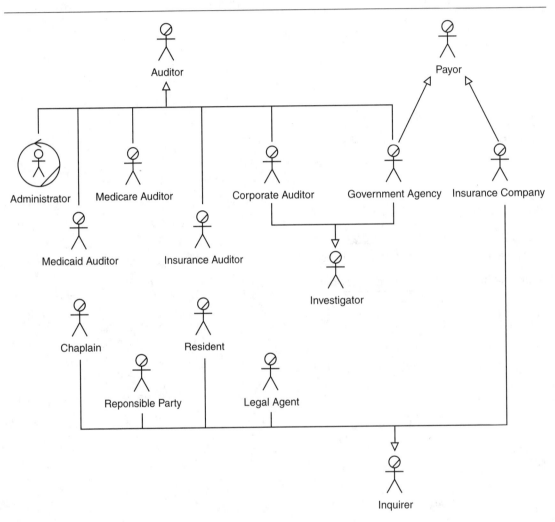

Figure A–47   Auditors and agents

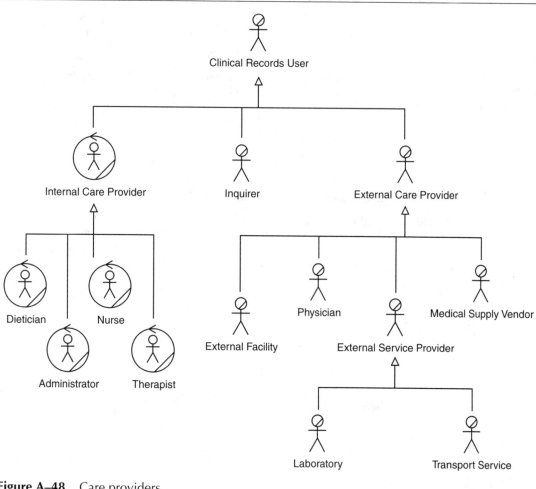

Figure A–48   Care providers

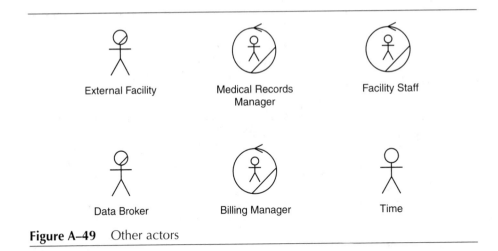

Figure A–49   Other actors

Use Cases

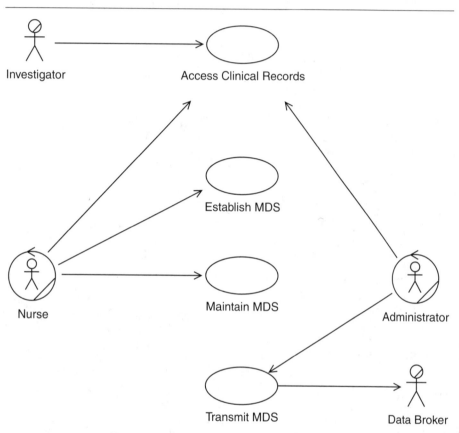

Figure A–50   Comply with Regulations use case diagram

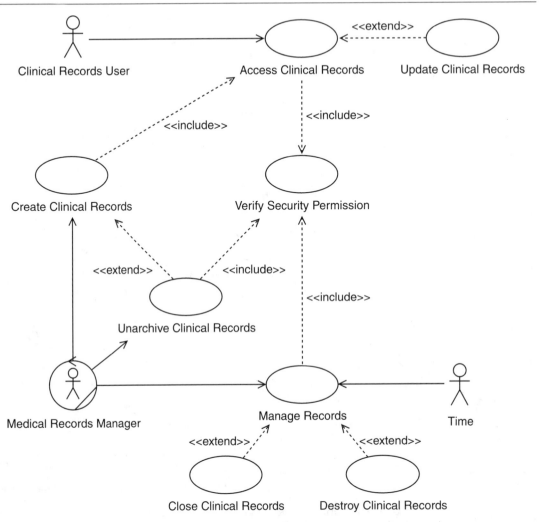

Figure A–51 Manage Clinical Records use case diagram

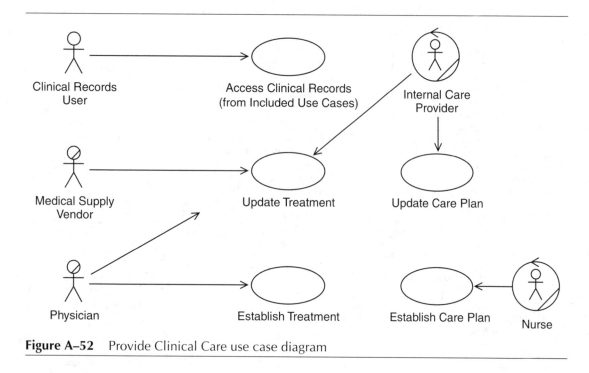

Figure A–52 Provide Clinical Care use case diagram

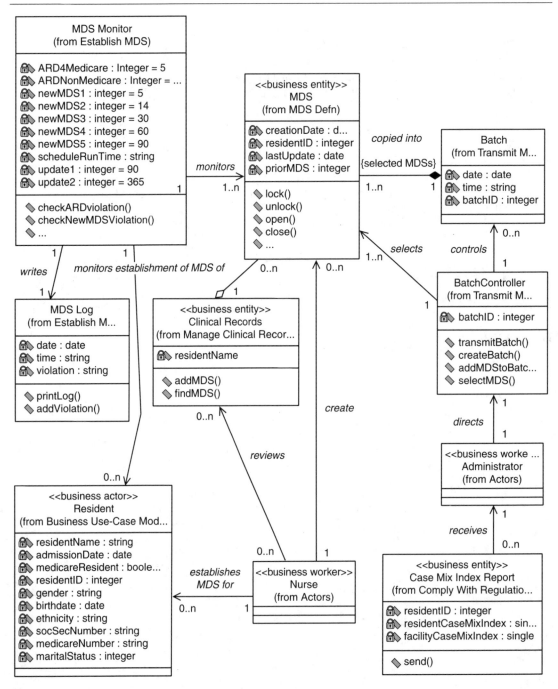

Figure A–53 Comply with Regulations class diagram

Comply with Regulations: Establish MDS

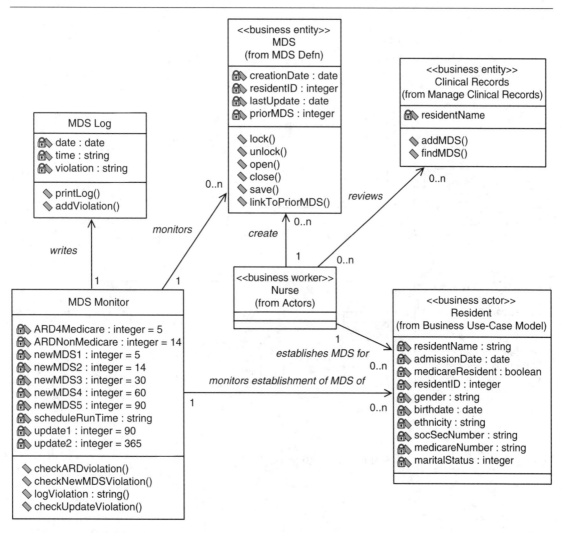

Figure A–54   Establish MDS class diagram

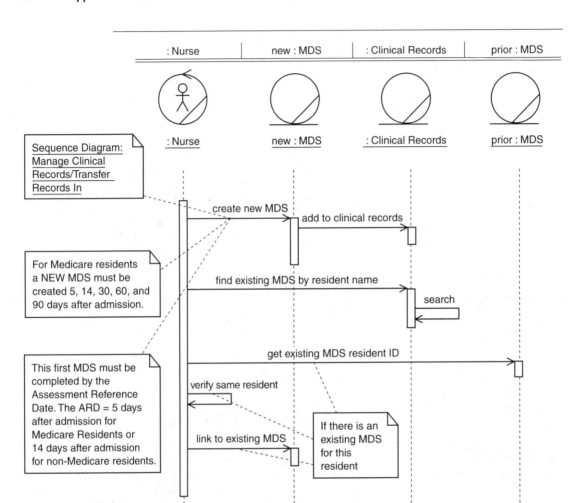

Figure A–55   Establish MDS sequence diagram

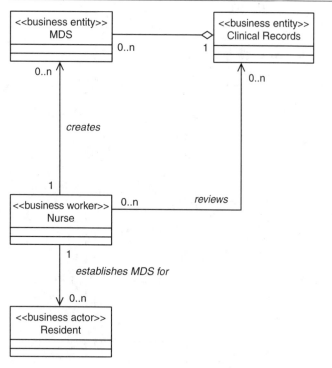

Figure A–56   Nurse view class diagram

Comply with Regulations: Maintain MDS

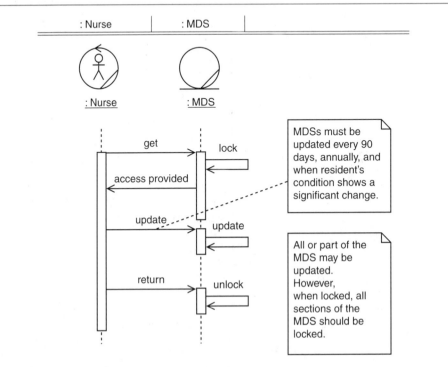

Figure A–57 Maintain MDS sequence diagram

Comply with Regulations: MDS Definition

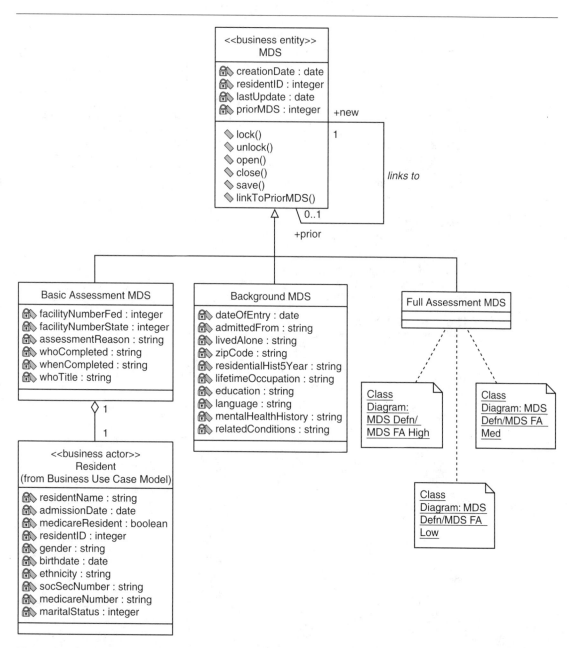

Figure A–58 MDS structure overview class diagram

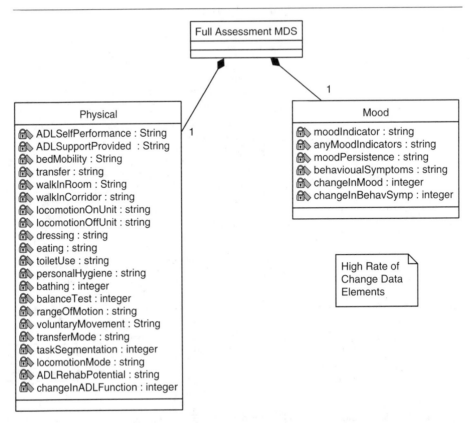

Figure A–59 MDS high-change elements class diagram

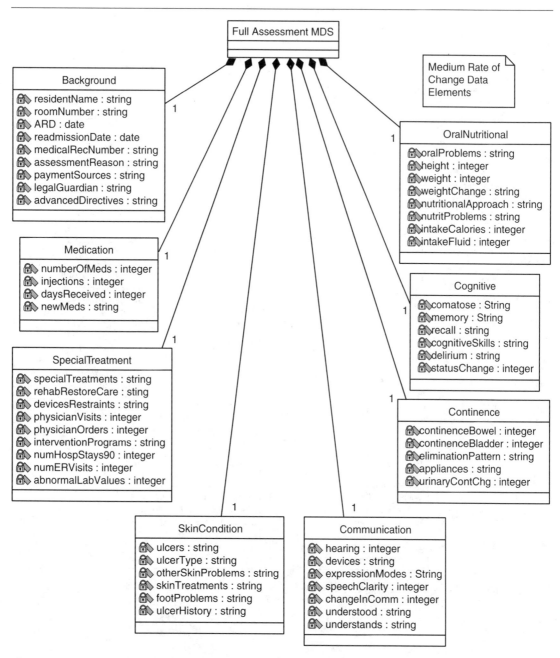

Figure A–60   MDS medium-change elements class diagram

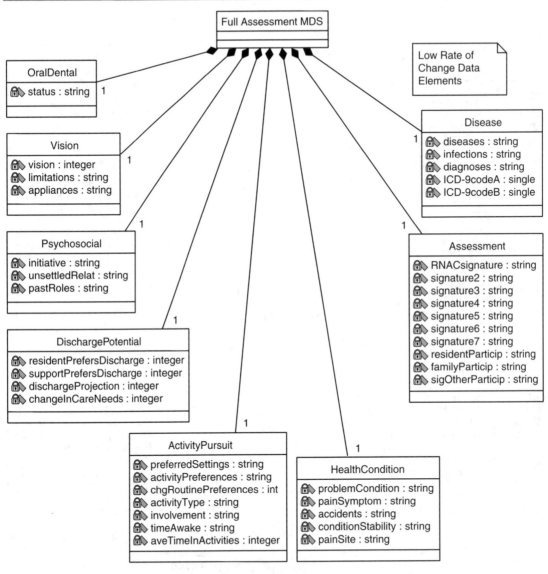

Figure A–61   MDS low-change elements class diagram

Comply with Regulations: Transmit MDS

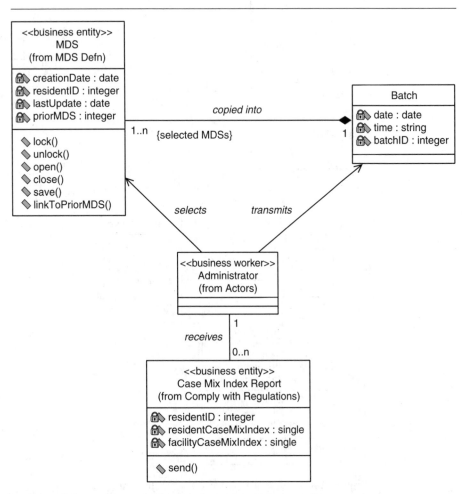

Figure A–62   Transmit MDS sequence diagram (initial)

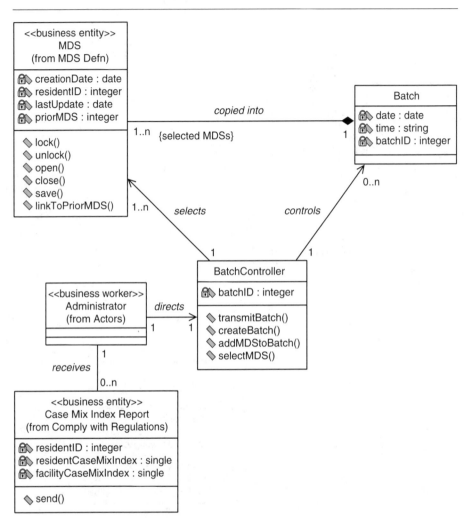

Figure A–63 Transmit MDS class diagram (revised)

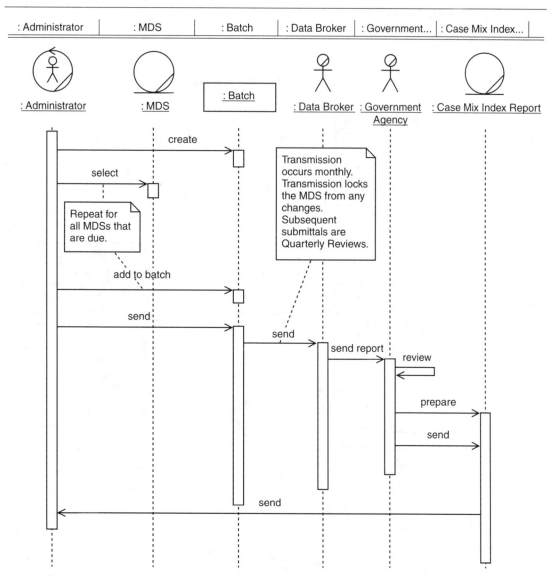

Figure A–64 Transmit MDS sequence diagram

Included Use Cases
Security Access

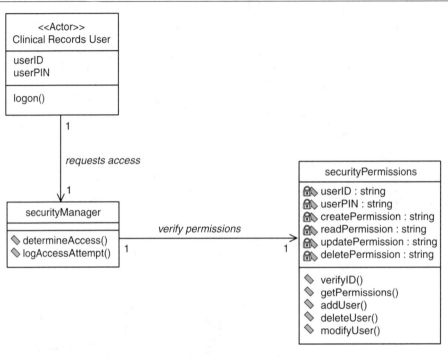

Figure A–65   Security Access class diagram

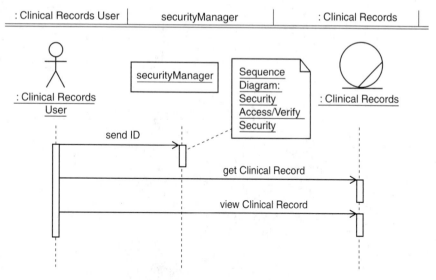

Figure A–66   Access Clinical Records sequence diagram

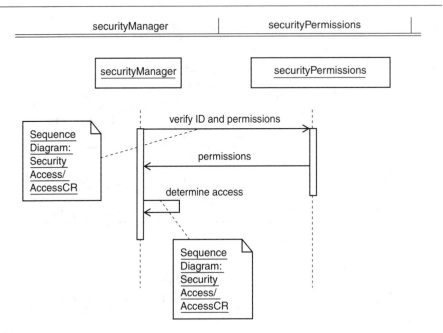

Figure A–67   Verify Security sequence diagram

The Database Design Models

Comply with Regulations

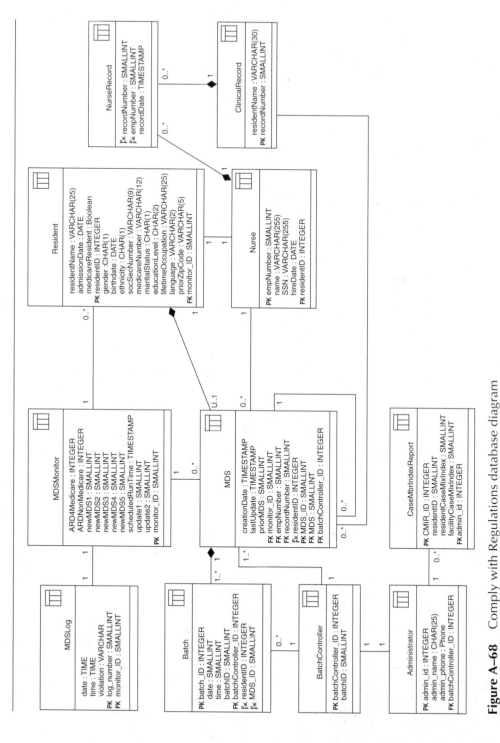

Figure A–68 Comply with Regulations database diagram

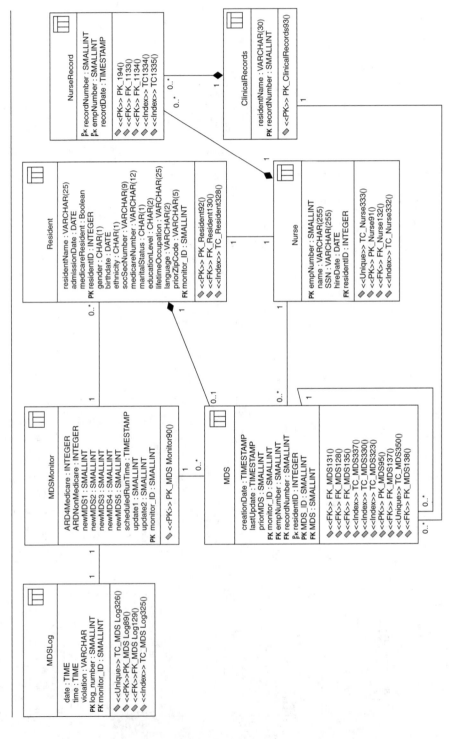

Figure A–69 Establish MDS database diagram

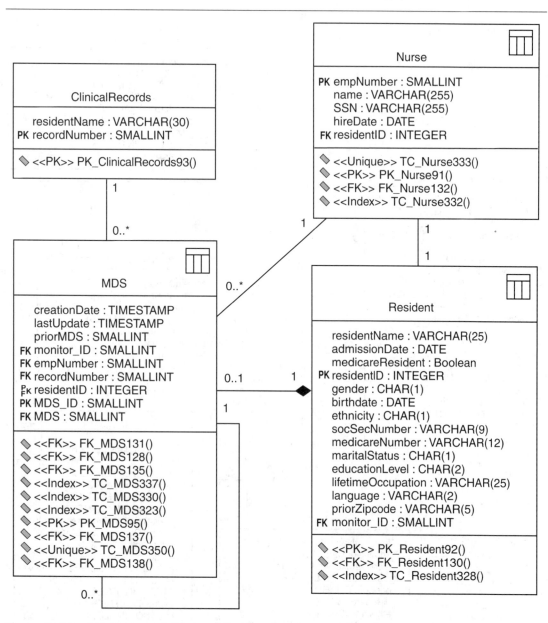

Figure A–70   Nurse view of database diagram

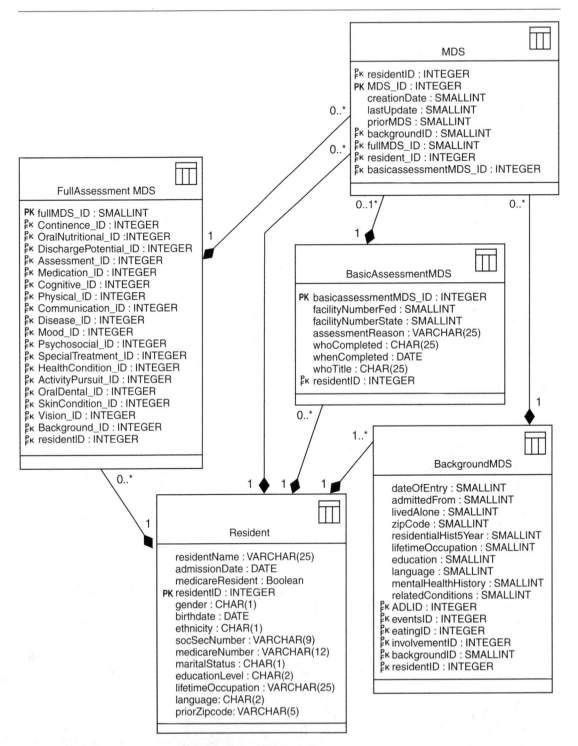

Figure A–71 MDS structure overview database diagram

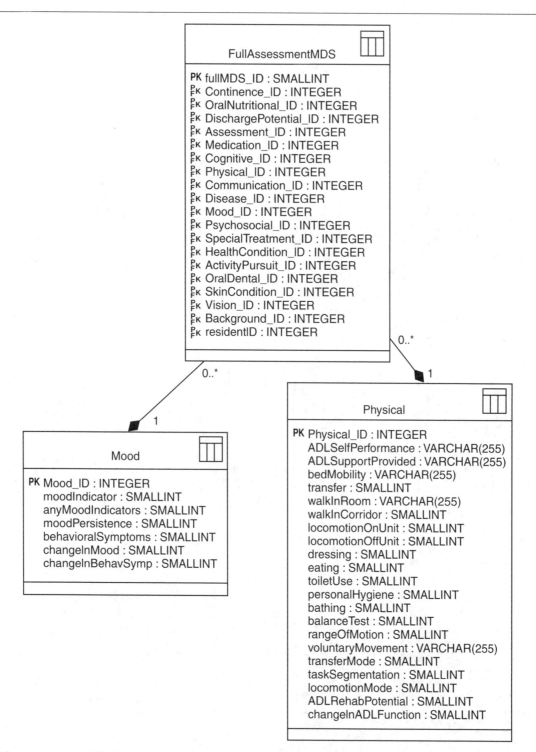

Figure A-72 MDS high-change elements database diagram

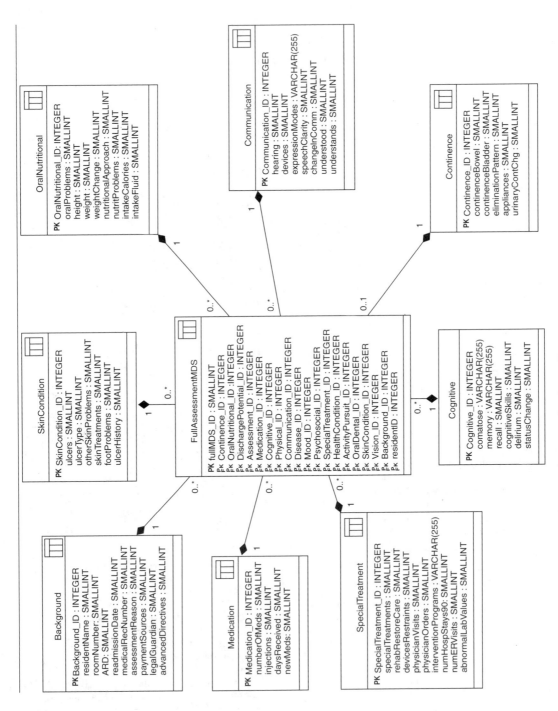

Figure A–73 MDS medium-change elements database diagram

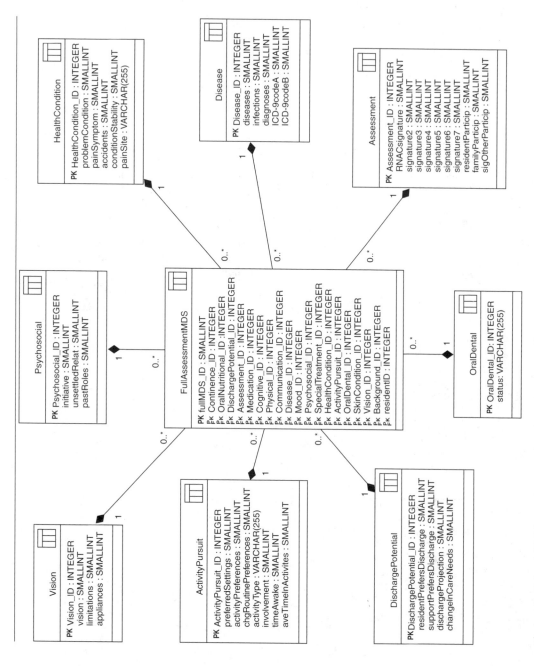

Figure A–74 MDS low-change elements database diagram

Comply with Regulations: Transmit MDS

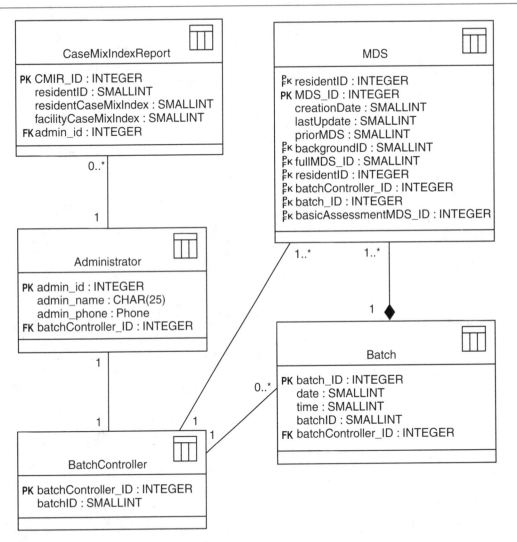

Figure A–75   Transmit MDS database diagram

Appendix B

Use Case Descriptions

This appendix contains various use case descriptions that provide more complete information on the project discussed in the EAB Healthcare case study. Some have been referenced in the previous text and some have not.

Use Case Description—OMaR Project

Use Case Name: **Access Clinical Records**

Use Case Purpose: The purpose of this use case is to allow the Clinical Record information to be accessed by the appropriate actors.

Point of Contact:

Date Modified:

Preconditions: None identified.

Postconditions: Clinical Records will remain locked until the Clinical Records User completes access and "releases" the Clinical Records.

Limitations: Only the same Clinical Records User to whom the Clinical Records were released can provide updates or return the Clinical Records.

Assumptions: None identified.

Basic Flow:

  A. The Clinical Records User identifies him- or herself to OMaR.

  B. INCLUSION: Perform Verify Security Permissions use case. OMaR verifies the Clinical Records User's security access, permissions, and so on.

  C. The Clinical Records User specifies the Clinical Record by Resident.

  D. The Clinical Record is made available for the Clinical Records User to view.

  E. If the Clinical Records User wants to update the Clinical Record, EXTENSION: Perform Update Clinical Records use case.

  F. If the Resident is being transferred out of the facility, update Records Closure Schedule and create a copy of the Clinical Records for the Clinical Records User.

  G. If the Clinical Records User wants to access additional records, go to step C.

Alternate Flow:

Condition Triggering Alternate Flow: OMaR does not recognize the Clinical Records User as having permission to review the Clinical Records.

  C1. Access to the Clinical Records is denied.

  C2. OMaR tells the Clinical Records User that he or she does not have sufficient permission to review the Clinical Records.

  C3. OMaR returns to step A in the Basic Flow.

Condition Triggering Alternate Flow: The requested Clinical Record is already being used and is locked out.

  C1. Access to the Clinical Records is denied.

  C2. OMaR tells the Clinical Records User that the Clinical Record requested is in use and locked out.

  C3. OMaR returns to step A in the Basic Flow.

Use Case Description—OMaR Project

Use Case Name: **Close Clinical Records**

Use Case Purpose: The purpose of this use case is to close (that is, allow no further updates) and archive the Clinical Records. This places the specific (based on Resident) Clinical Records out of daily use.

Point of Contact:
Date Modified:

Preconditions: The Manage Clinical Records use case has been executed.

Postconditions: The Records Closure Schedule and Records Destruction Schedule may be updated.

Limitations: None identified.

Assumptions: This use case will be automatically executed once a day, between 12:00 A.M. and 4:00 A.M. This use case can also be invoked by the Medical Records Manager.

Record Destruction Date is set for 7 years (default) after closure.

Clinical Records are to be closed 14 days after the Resident leaves the facility.

Basic Flow:
A. All Clinical Records are examined for each Resident to determine whether the Resident is deceased or has left the facility.
B. For all deceased Residents, the Clinical Records for those Residents are closed (that is, locked against update) and are added to the Records Closure Schedule for immediate closure.
C. For all Residents who have left, the Clinical Records for those Residents are added to the Records Closure Schedule for scheduled closure.
D. All Clinical Records scheduled for closure are moved to the Archive.
E. The Records Closure Schedule is updated to reflect the closures.
F. The Records Destruction Schedule is updated for each of the newly closed Clinical Records.

Alternate Flow:
Condition Triggering Alternate Flow: None identified.

Use Case Description—OMaR Project

Use Case Name: **Create Clinical Record**

Use Case Purpose: The purpose of this use case is to create a new Clinical Record for a Resident.

Point of Contact:
Date Modified:

Preconditions: None identified.
Postconditions: A new Clinical Record is created.

Limitations: None identified.
Assumptions: The incoming Clinical Record information is in the same or compatible format as that used in the OMaR system. If not, the information will have to be entered by hand.

Basic Flow:
- A. INCLUSION: Perform Access Clinical Records use case.
- B. The actor searches the Clinical Records to determine if the Resident has been in the Facility before. If the records are not found the actor searches the Archive. If the Resident is not found in either, the Resident is considered to be new to the Facility.
- C. If the Resident is new to the facility, the actor creates an Internal Clinical Record and copies/enters the External Clinical Record information. Then this use case ends.
- D. If the Resident has been in the facility before, and if the records are closed, EXTENSION: Perform Unarchive Clinical Records use case.
- E. The actor creates an Internal Clinical Record and copies/enters the External Clinical Record information.
- F. The actor then links the Internal Clinical Record to the closed Clinical Records via the Clinical Records case number from the closed records.
- G. If the Resident has been in the Facility before, and if the records are not closed, remove the Clinical Records from the Records Closure Schedule.
- H. The actor copies/enters incoming External Clinical Record information into the open Internal Clinical Records.

Alternate Flow:
Condition Triggering Alternate Flow: None identified.

Use Case Description—OMaR Project

Use Case Name: **Destroy Clinical Records**

Use Case Purpose: The purpose of this use case is to implement the destruction of Clinical Records that have been held in the Archive for a specified period of time.

Point of Contact:

Date Modified:

Preconditions: The Manage Clinical Records use case has been executed and the Close Clinical Records use case has been executed.

Postconditions: The Records Destruction Schedule may be updated.

Limitations: This use case should be executed after the execution of the Close Clinical Records use case.

Assumptions: This use case will be automatically executed once a day, between 12:00 A.M. and 4:00 A.M. This use case can also be invoked by the Medical Records Manager.

Record Destruction Date is set for 7 years (default) after closure.

Basic Flow:

    A.   The Records Destruction Schedule is examined to determine which Clinical Records are scheduled for destruction.

    B.   If any records are scheduled for destruction, the Archive is opened with exclusive access. If not, this use case terminates.

    C.   All Clinical Records due for destruction are deleted from the Archive.

    D.   The Archive is closed and exclusive access is released.

    E.   The Records Destruction Schedule is updated to reflect the destruction of the Clinical Records.

Alternate Flow:

    Condition Triggering Alternate Flow: None identified.

Use Case Description—OMaR Project

Use Case Name:	**Establish Care Plan**
Use Case Purpose:	The purpose of this use case is to create a new Care Plan for a Resident.

Point of Contact:
Date Modified:

Preconditions:	The Access Clinical Records use case has been successfully executed.
Postconditions:	A Care Plan is created.

Limitations:	A Care Plan must be created within 24 hours of Resident's admission.
Assumptions:	None identified.

Basic Flow:
- A.   The Nurse reviews the Clinical Records via the Access Clinical Records use case.
- B.   The Nurse extracts the needed information from the Clinical Records to create a new Care Plan.
- C.   The Nurse updates the Care Plan Review Schedule.

Alternate Flow:
Condition Triggering Alternate Flow: None identified.

Use Case Description—OMaR Project

Use Case Name:	**Establish MDS**
Use Case Purpose:	The purpose of this use case is to create a new MDS for a newly admitted Resident.

Point of Contact:
Date Modified:

Preconditions:	Existing Clinical Records have been transferred to the Facility. The Access Clinical Records use case has been successfully executed.
Postconditions:	A new MDS is created.
Limitations:	This first MDS must be completed by the Assessment Reference Date (ARD). The ARD = 5 days after admission for Medicare Residents or 14 days after admission for non-Medicare Residents. For Medicare Residents a new MDS must be created 5, 14, 30, 60, and 90 days after admission.
Assumptions:	None identified.

Basic Flow:

    A. The Nurse reviews the Clinical Records via the Access Clinical Records use case.

    B. If there is no new MDS, the Nurse creates a new MDS for this Resident.

    C. The Nurse adds the newly created MDS to the Clinical Records.

Alternate Flow:

Condition Triggering Alternate Flow: The new MDS is not created prior to the ARD or, for a Medicare Resident, a new MDS was not created at the appropriate times (see limitations) after admission.

    A. This use case will not be modified by these conditions. A process will be run daily (during third shift). This process will report on any such MDS creation/ update violations.

Use Case Description—OMaR Project

Use Case Name:	**Establish Treatment**
Use Case Purpose:	The purpose of this use case is to create or update a Treatment for a Resident.

Point of Contact:
Date Modified:

Preconditions:	The Access Clinical Records use case has been successfully executed.
Postconditions:	Treatment is established.
Limitations:	None identified.
Assumptions:	None identified.

Basic Flow:

    A.   The Physician reviews the Clinical Records via the Access Clinical Records use case.

    B.   The Physician writes Orders to implement the Treatment.

Alternate Flow:

    Condition Triggering Alternate Flow: None identified.

Use Case Description—OMaR Project

Use Case Name: **Maintain MDS**

Use Case Purpose: The purpose of this use case is to keep MDSs updated.

Point of Contact:
Date Modified:

Preconditions: The Access Clinical Records use case has been successfully executed.
Postconditions: The MDS is updated.

Limitations: The MDS must be updated
(a) Every 90 days
(b) Annually
(c) When the Resident has shown a significant change in condition
Assumptions: None identified.

Basic Flow:
A. The Nurse reviews the Clinical Records via the Access Clinical Records use case.
B. The Nurse assesses the Resident's condition.
C. The Nurse updates the MDS if required (see limitations above).
D. The Nurse releases the MDS.
E. The Nurse repeats this process for each Resident that is assigned to the Nurse.

Alternate Flow:
Condition Triggering Alternate Flow: The new MDS is not updated prior to the required times (see limitations).
A. See the Alternate Flow of the Establish MDS use case.

Use Case Description—OMaR Project

Use Case Name: **Manage Clinical Records**

Use Case Purpose: The purpose of this use case is to automate many of the tasks that are performed by the Medical Records Manager (for example, closure and destruction of the Clinical Records).

Point of Contact:

Date Modified:

Preconditions: The Access Clinical Records use case has been successfully executed.

Postconditions: The Records Destruction Schedule and/or the Records Closure Schedule may be updated.

Limitations: None identified.

Assumptions: This use case will be automatically executed once a day, between 12:00 A.M. and 4:00 A.M. An actor can also manually initiate this use case.

Basic Flow:

    A.   The Time actor or the Medical Records Manager actor activates this use case.

    B.   INCLUSION: Perform Verify Security Permissions use case.

    C.   EXTENSION: Perform Close Clinical Records use case.

    D.   EXTENSION: Perform Destroy Clinical Records use case.

Alternate Flow:

    Condition Triggering Alternate Flow: None identified.

Use Case Description—OMaR Project

Use Case Name: **Transmit MDS**

Use Case Purpose: The purpose of this use case is to submit the MDSs of all Residents to the Government Agency responsible for reviewing the MDSs for compliance with regulations.

Point of Contact:
Date Modified:

Preconditions: The Access Clinical Records use case has been successfully executed.
Postconditions: Submittal locks each MDS submitted from further changes. Subsequent submittals of MDSs that were previously submitted are Reviews of those MDSs or are to correct a "bad" transmission.

Limitations: The submittal of new MDSs must occur monthly.
Assumptions: None identified.

Basic Flow:

    A. For those MDSs (and Quarterly Updates) that are due for submittal, the Administrator (through delegation to the Facility Staff) prepares these MDSs for submittal.

    B. The MDSs are electronically submitted to the Data Broker.

    C. The Data Broker reviews the MDSs for correctness, completeness, and so on.

    D. The Data Broker sends the results of this analysis to the Government Agency.

    E. The Government Agency prepares a Case Mix Index Report based on the MDSs and the Data Broker's analysis.

    F. The Government Agency sends the Case Mix Index Report to the Administrator.

Alternate Flow:

    Condition Triggering Alternate Flow: None identified.

Use Case Description—OMaR Project

Use Case Name: **Unarchive Clinical Records**

Use Case Purpose: The purpose of this use case is to recover Clinical Records from the Archive.

Point of Contact:
Date Modified:

Preconditions: None identified.

Postconditions: The Records Closure Schedule and Records Destruction Schedule may be updated.

Limitations: The Clinical Records to be recovered are specified by Resident.

Assumptions: Clinical Records are to be closed 14 days after the Resident leaves the Facility.

Basic Flow:

  A. The Archive is locked against update.
  B. The specified Clinical Record is searched for in the Records Destruction Schedule.
  C. The Records Destruction Schedule is updated to remove the requested Clinical Record from the Schedule.
  D. The specified Clinical Record is recovered from the Archive.
  E. If the Resident has left the facility, the Records Closure Schedule is updated to schedule the Clinical Record for closure.
  F. The Archive is closed and exclusive access is released.

Alternate Flow:

  Condition Triggering Alternate Flow: The specified Clinical Record is not found in the Records Destruction Schedule.

  B1. An error message is displayed to the user and also logged, indicating the specific Clinical Record was not found in the Records Destruction Schedule.
  B2. Step F in the Basic Flow is then executed.

  Condition Triggering Alternate Flow: The specified Clinical Record is not found in the Archive.

  D1. An error message is displayed to the user and also logged, indicating the specific Clinical Record was not found in the Archive.
  D2. Step F in the Basic Flow is then executed.

Use Case Description—OMaR Project

Use Case Name: **Update Care Plan**
Use Case Purpose: The purpose of this use case is to update a Care Plan for a Resident.

Point of Contact:
Date Modified:

Preconditions: The Access Clinical Records use case has been successfully executed.
Postconditions: Care Plan is updated.

Limitations: None identified.
Assumptions: None identified.

Basic Flow:
- A. The actor reviews the Clinical Records via the Access Clinical Records use case.
- B. The actor assesses the implementation of Orders.
- C. The actor updates Progress Notes and Addendum if needed.
- D. The actor recommends Treatment if appropriate.
- E. The actor transcribes Orders from Clinical Records into the Care Plan.

Alternate Flow:
Condition Triggering Alternate Flow: None identified.

Use Case Description—OMaR Project

Use Case Name: **Update Clinical Records**

Use Case Purpose: The purpose of this use case is to update a Clinical Record's data.

Point of Contact:
Date Modified:

Preconditions: The Access Clinical Records use case has been successfully executed.

Postconditions: The Clinical Record is updated.

Limitations: None identified.

Assumptions: None identified.

Basic Flow:

A. The Clinical Records User requests to update a specific Resident's Clinical Record.

B. The Clinical Record is retrieved.

C. The Clinical Records User updates the Clinical Record.

Alternate Flow:

Condition Triggering Alternate Flow: The update of the Clinical Record fails.

C1. OMaR tells the Clinical Records User that the update has failed.

C2. The use case continues at step A of the Basic Flow, where the Clinical Records User can try again or end the use case.

Use Case Description—OMaR Project

Use Case Name: **Update Treatment**
Use Case Purpose: The purpose of this use case is to update the Treatment for a Resident.

Point of Contact:
Date Modified:

Preconditions: The Access Clinical Records use case has been successfully executed.
Postconditions: The treatment is updated.

Limitations: Based on security privileges the actor's ability to change Treatment varies.
Assumptions: None identified.

Basic Flow:
- A. The actor reviews the Clinical Records via the Access Clinical Records use case.
- B. The actor authorizes recommended Treatments if appropriate.
- C. The actor recommends new Treatments.
- D. The actor reviews recommended Orders.
- E. The actor authorizes recommended Orders.
- F. The actor reviews test results.
- G. The actor writes new Treatments and related Orders.
- H. The actor updates Progress Notes if applicable.

Alternate Flow:
Condition Triggering Alternate Flow: None identified.

Use Case Description—OMaR Project

Use Case Name: **Verify Security Permissions**

Use Case Purpose: The purpose of this use case is to verify that the actor requesting access to Clinical Records information is permitted to have access to such information. This use case is "included" in other use cases.

Point of Contact:

Date Modified:

Preconditions: None identified.

Postconditions: None identified

Limitations: None identified.

Assumptions: None identified.

Basic Flow:

    A. The actor enters identification information.

    B. The actor's identity is verified.

    C. The actor's permission set is retrieved.

    D. The actor's permission set is provided to the "including" use case.

Alternate Flow:

Condition Triggering Alternate Flow: OMaR does not recognize the actor as having access to the system.

    A1. If verification of the actor identification has failed three times, OMaR will disable this data entry interface. OMaR logs these attempts in the security log. This use case then terminates.

    A2. If verification of the actor's identification has not yet failed three times, OMaR asks the actor to reenter identification.

    A3. OMaR returns to step A in the Basic Flow.

Glossary

Activity diagram   A diagram showing the flow of activities. Used to give a high-level view of a business process.

Actor   An external person or system that interfaces with (that is, uses or is used by) the system. Depicts a user's logical role.

Aggregation   A relationship between model elements indicating that one element is a "part of" another element (aggregate).

ANSI   American National Standards Institute.

Association   A relationship between two model elements.

Association class   A class that embodies properties of an association (typically an association between two other classes).

Attribute   The properties of a class.

Business actor   An actor that is external to the business.

Business entity   Something used by a business worker while fulfilling a use case.

Business model   A model that describes the business operation. The business model is composed of the business use case model and the business object model.

Business object model   An object model that provides the realization of a business use case. An internal view of the business.

Business use case   A use case, initiated by a business actor, that the business performs.

Business use case model   A use case model that describes the business functions from a business actor's point of view. An external view of the business.

Business worker   An actor that is internal to the business whose work helps realize a business use case.

Candidate key   A column or set of columns that uniquely identifies a row in a table.

Class diagram   A diagram that shows classes, their interrelationships, and their relationships with other model elements. The intent is to show the basic structure of the system.

Component diagram   A diagram for database design that depicts physical storage of the database, including the DBMS, tablespaces, and partitions. Can also include applications and their interfaces to each other and to database elements.

Conceptual model   A very high-level model of a system or database. Typically this model contains high-level domain entities and their basic relationships with other major domain entities. Its main purpose is to define the scope of the system. This model should be technology independent.

Constraint   A rule that limits the value of or actions on the specified data field.

Control class   An active class that controls the behavior of one or more other classes.

Data dictionary   When referring to databases, a file or files that contain information describing the data in the database; also called a system catalog.

Database   A collection of information.

Database diagram   A diagram depicting the structure of the database, including tables, columns, constraints, and so on.

DBMS   Database management system.

DDL   Data Definition Language.

Denormalization   A process applied to a database schema that reduces its level of normalization. Used to improve the operational effectiveness (for example, simplified access, better performance, and so on) of the database.

Deployment diagram   A diagram depicting the hardware configuration that is used for the database and applications.

Derived attribute   An attribute whose value is determined by the value of other attributes.

Domain   The valid set of values for an attribute or column.

Entity   An object in the business or system.

Entity-relationship diagram   A diagram depicting entities and their relationships with each other.

ER   Entity-relationship.

Extends   A stereotype of a relationship that indicates an optional use case flow that may be executed, based on specific criteria.

Extension point   Location in the flow of events of a use case where the use case is extended by another use case.

Foreign key   A column or set of columns within a table that map to the primary key of another table.

Functional decomposition   An approach to systems development in which the larger system is broken down into smaller parts. Those parts may then be broken down into even smaller parts, and so on. Each part of the system that is so decomposed is an aggregate of its smaller parts.

Generalization   A relationship between model elements indicating that one element (subclass) is a "type of" another element (superclass).

Identifying relationship   A relationship between two tables in which the child table must coexist with the parent table.

Includes   A stereotype of a relationship that indicates a use case flow that is inserted into another use case or use cases.

Inclusion point   Location in the flow of events of a use case where another use case is inserted into the flow of the original use case.

Index   A file that enables faster data access.

Inheritance   The mechanism by which more-specific elements incorporate the structure and behavior of more general elements.

Interaction diagram   Sequence and/or collaboration diagrams, both of which show the interaction of objects within the system. Can be used to understand queries that will affect the database and even build indexes based on the information modeled.

Key migration   A process whereby the primary key of a table is added as a foreign key to a related table.

Logical design   An analysis/design-level model of a system or database. Its main purpose is to define architecture and overall design of the system.

MDS   Minimum Data Set. A standard collection of information about a resident who is being cared for in a healthcare facility.

Non-identifying relationship   A relationship between two tables in which each table can exist independently of the other.

Normalization   An analytical technique used to produce a correct relational database design.

Package   A UML element used to group other elements together.

Partition   A division of storage space.

Passive class   A class that is not active and does not embody any control of the system.

Physical model   A detailed implementation-level model of a system or database. Its main purpose is to define the specific, detailed implementation of the system.

Postcondition   Possible states of the system that exist after the execution of a use case.

Precondition   The required state of the system, or conditions that must be true, for a use case to be executed.

Primary key   The candidate key that is chosen to identify rows in a table.

Profile   An extension to the UML that uses stereotypes and tagged values to extend the UML for specialized purposes while keeping the UML metamodel intact.

RDBMS   Relational database management system.

Referential integrity   A rule that states if a foreign key exists in a table, its value must be null or must also appear in a related table's candidate key.

Relationship   An association between tables.

Requirement   A statement describing a desired capability of the system.

Role   A set of behaviors of an element specific to its interaction with other elements in a given situation.

Schema   A description of a database's structure.

Sequence diagram   A diagram of collaborating objects and the messages they send to each other arranged in time order. Sequence diagrams show how use cases are realized.

SQL   Structured Query Language.

Statechart   A diagram that captures the dynamic behavior of a class or part of the system.

Stereotype   A specialized version of a standard UML element.

Stored procedure   An independent procedural function that typically executes on the server.

Swimlane   A vertical delimiter on an activity diagram used to partition the activities performed by specific responsible parties.

Tablespace A construct representing an amount of storage space that is to be allocated to tables, indexes, and so on.

Tagged value Allows additional information about a standard UML element to be specified.

Transaction An operation or series of operations applied against a database.

Trigger A procedural function designed to execute when a table is modified.

UML Unified Modeling Language.

Use case A complete flow of actions initiated by an actor that the system performs, which provide value to that actor.

Use case diagram A diagram that shows use cases and their relationships with actors and other use cases. The use case model is a model of the system's intended functions and its environment, which supports the business processes. This model serves as a contract between the customer and the developers.

View A virtual table that, from the user's perspective, behaves exactly like a typical table but has no independent existence of its own.

Bibliography

Blaha, Michael, and William Premerlani. 1998. *Object-Oriented Modeling and Design for Database Applications.* Upper Saddle River, NJ: Prentice Hall.

Booch, Grady, James Rumbaugh, and Ivar Jacobson. 1999. *The Unified Modeling Language User Guide.* Reading, MA: Addison-Wesley.

Conallen, Jim. 2000. *Building Web Applications with UML*. Boston: Addison-Wesley.

Gamma, Eric, et al. 1995. *Design Patterns: Elements of Reusable Object-Oriented Software*. Reading, MA: Addison-Wesley.

Jacobson, Ivar, Maria Ericsson, and Agenta Jacobson. 1995. *The Object Advantage: Business Process Reengineering with Object Technology.* Reading, MA: Addison-Wesley.

Kruchten, Philippe. 1999. *The Rational Unified Process: An Introduction*. Reading, MA: Addison-Wesley.

Leffingwell, Dean, and Don Widrig. 2000. *Managing Software Requirements.* Boston: Addison-Wesley.

O'Neil, Patrick, and Elizabeth O'Neil. 2001. *Database Principles, Programming, and Performance*. San Francisco: Morgan Kaufmann.

Quatrani, Terry. 2000. *Visual Modeling with Rational Rose 2000 and UML.* Boston: Addison-Wesley.

Royce, Walker. 1999. *Software Project Management*. Reading, MA: Addison-Wesley.

Rumbaugh, James, et al. 1991. *Object-Oriented Modeling and Design.* Englewood Cliffs, NJ: Prentice Hall.

Rumbaugh, James, Ivar Jacobson, and Grady Booch. 1998. *The Unified Modeling Language Reference Manual.* Reading, MA: Addison-Wesley.

Schneider, Geri, and Jason P. Winters. 1998. *Applying Use Cases: A Practical Guide.* Reading, MA: Addison-Wesley.

Taylor, Allen G. 1998. *SQL for Dummies.* Foster City, CA: IDG Books.

Vaskevitch, David. 1993. *Client/Server Strategies.* San Francisco: IDG Books.

Index

Note: Page numbers followed by letters *f* and *t* indicate figures and tables, respectively.

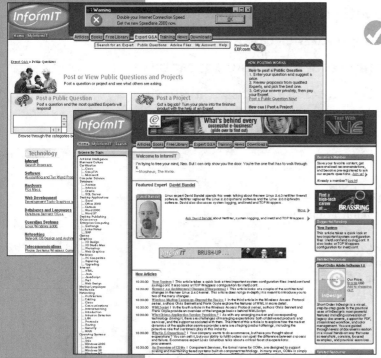